UNARMED

UNARMED

De-Escalation Techniques to Cultivate Courage, Compassion, and Connection

Joe Smarro

Published by Game Changer Publishing

Paperback ISBN: 978-1-963793-24-6
Hardcover ISBN: 978-1-963793-25-3
Digital: ISBN: 978-1-963793-26-0

www.GameChangerPublishing.com

DEDICATION

To all who wander in search of stories that resonate
in their soul, this is for you.

To every therapist who has guided my healing
journey, thank you.

To anyone I have personally hurt, I am sorry for
not knowing better sooner.

To all first responders trying your best, I love you.

For those who see me and still love me, thank you.

Read This First

To say thanks for buying and reading my book, I would like to offer you a **FREE** online course for Effective Communication and Active Listening. (A $97 value)

To Download Your Free Video, Scan the QR Code:
This will link you to an online video of the Effective
Communication and Active Listening course.

UNARMED

De-Escalation Techniques to Cultivate
Courage, Compassion, and Connection

Joe Smarro

www.GameChangerPublishing.com

Foreword

By: Jesse Trevino

I met Joseph Smarro in the fall of 2000 while serving in the United States Marine Corps. I had recently been medically cleared from an injury I sustained and hid during the dreaded Crucible. The Crucible is the final Marine Corps boot camp test, a grueling 54-hour training evolution every recruit must successfully negotiate to become a Marine. On day one of this event, I knew I was injured. Stubbornly, I refused to disclose my injury, choosing instead to endure and finish. While I wish I could attribute my determination to grit or courage, my true motivation came from never wanting to repeat such an experience. I just wanted to complete the final test, and I did. I became a Marine.

Once back in garrison, I finally disclosed my injury and sought treatment. Turns out my foot was broken. As a result, I had to stay at the Marine Corps Recruit Depot to heal while my platoon moved on without me. Often, our perspectives on life events are short-sighted. At the time, this news was devastating. I could not have known then what the universe had in store for me.

Eventually, I was medically cleared to join the fleet and assigned to a new training cohort. That is when I met my first roommate, Joseph Alfred Smarro, this smiling, sarcastic, funny kid from New York. I guess some things never really change. Looking back on 23 years of friendship, I am grateful for that purposefully placed serendipitous, albeit painful, blessing. If not for that injury, I likely would have never met Joe Smarro.

Since then, life has positioned me with a unique vantage point of Joe's life. I have observed him operate through both personal and professional lenses, though I am not sure which of the two is more impressive. Our experiences over the last two decades exceed what most people will ever go through in a lifetime. We shared a fighting hole in Iraq. We both served on the San Antonio Police Department's celebrated Mental Health Unit. We both obtained academic and professional achievements. We founded the international consulting and training firm SolutionPoint+ together. We did all of this while navigating life through marriages, kids, divorces, mental health diagnoses, failures, and wins. I have watched my friend take these collective experiences and use them to grow into the resilient, wise leader he is today.

Many of the lessons he learned are now bestowed on you in this book. As I write these words, I am filled with excitement. My excitement comes from knowing what this book will do for anyone who chooses to apply Joe's principles. As you turn the pages, you, too, will get to know my friend, at least to some degree, as I have. I encourage you to learn from him.

As a criminologist and former police detective, I believe this book (at the very least) is a well-thought-out mapping of the de-escalation process. This human behavior GPS navigation system, if you will, was developed using various sources such as neuroscience, social science, Joe's life challenges, and most of all, a collection of learnings from his time in the Mental Health Unit (MHU). It was in this unit that Joe discovered his superpower: forging human connection.

I followed Joe into policing after the economic crisis of 2008. I thought I knew the kind of cop I wanted to be. Misguided, I was taking my trauma out on society. I wanted to fix the world, or what happened to me in childhood, by arresting "bad guys." Fortunately for me and the community I worked in, Joe rescued me from myself.

Recruited by Joe, I went reluctantly to the MHU, a unit he had already been on for a few years. Teaching de-escalation or talking to people in crisis was not my idea of sexy policing. I had no shortage of ignorance back then. Moreover, I had been estranged from Joe for some time. Life, my mental illness, and trauma avoidance had kept us apart. We still considered each other friends, but we lived separate lives. When he offered me the MHU opportunity, I jumped at the chance. Not only would I get to use the skills I learned in graduate school, but I would finally get to work with my Marine Corps buddy again.

Working there brought many surprises. I found the importance of mental wellness. Crisis work intrigued me. The biggest surprise was discovering how fantastic Joe was at de-escalating people, even in the most dynamic of public safety situations.

The Joe I remember from our days in the Corps was this immature, heckling, smart-ass, cocky Marine. He was the platoon clown for those who knew him well; leadership knew him as a disciplined and stoic tactician under fire. This new "Mental Health Unit Joe" was unfamiliar to me. He was empathetic, steady, confident, and patient. For the years I was there, I watched and learned from the master.

In the field, Joe could get the most enraged and violent human to melt like ice cream in the Texas sun. Afterward, without fail, they would unburden themselves, trusting him to provide renewed hope in the midst of their suffering. I witnessed him sit with people who were tired and void of hope, craving the finality of death. People always opened up to him in their darkest, worst moments, accepting his helping hand. I would sit in awe, analogously reminded of Michelangelo's The Creation of Adam on the ceiling of the

Sistine Chapel. That is, I saw people granted hope for life through the extension of a helping hand; I also witnessed a virtuoso exhibit his refined, masterful life-saving skills.

Based on what you have read thus far, it may be easy to assume that Joe is not a fighter, but you would be wrong. Perhaps of all the "Joe moments" that were astonishing to me, the one that stays with me the most was when Joe told a deputy chief of a 2,500-person police department an unvarnished truth: their views on mental health were a clear example of why police officers who are suffering in silence would rather die by suicide than ever ask for help. This particular "leader" had previously told Joe that suicidal officers are weak and do not deserve to wear the badge. If you work in public safety, you can understand why Joe speaking up was so astonishing to me. He always risked being punished for insubordination to make sure toxic culture was called out. He championed officer mental wellness no matter the cost. And as far as his policing career is concerned, it cost him plenty. I admire his candor to this day.

I encourage you to read this book and apply its philosophies. Trust that the lessons compiled in the forthcoming pages will benefit your life, probably in ways you never considered. In this book, a de-escalation framework is provided by a person with many titles: TEDx speaker, author, HBO Emmy Award-winning documentary film subject, keynote speaker, "SeeEO," entrepreneur, and mental health advocate, to name a few. But the title I am most honored by and proud of is that Joe Smarro is my best friend. Thank you, and please enjoy.

Table of Contents

Introduction

*U*narmed is not just a title; it is a philosophy, a way of being. In our tumultuous world, which seems more divided and polarized than ever before, misunderstanding is rampant. It has never been more important for us to develop a deeper understanding of ourselves first and then each other.

As a combat-decorated Marine Corps veteran, celebrated former police officer in San Antonio, Texas, and survivor of childhood trauma, this book is the culmination of my experiences from the battlefields in the Middle East to the streets of South Texas. I want to share my triumphant journey from self-induced suffering to embracing the power of introspection. I hope that this book will become a universal guide for encouraging empathy, fostering resilience, and obtaining genuine connection.

My narrative, like so many, is one of stark contrast. I was trained as a warrior, yet I'm also a healer and mental health whisperer, molded by personal trauma and the discipline of military and police service. From my childhood, marred by abuse and abandonment, to the rigors of the Marine Corps, to confronting the complex challenges of policing and mental health advocacy, every chapter of my life has shaped my profound understanding of human behavior and the critical importance of empathy.

My experiences have led me to a pivotal realization: true strength comes from our capacity for self-awareness, compassion, acceptance, and connection – not the weapons we bear. This book is an invitation to explore these qualities to understand how empathy, emotional intelligence, and introspection can transform how we understand and interact with ourselves and others. It also serves as a skills-based guide to help you master de-escalation techniques, not only in a crisis context as a first responder but as a fundamental approach to navigating all of life's internal and external conflicts.

Unarmed drives to the heart of what it means to be a leader – in your community, corporation, agency, or family. It leverages lessons from Stoicism and my therapeutic journey to go beyond the traditional discourse on emotional intelligence. The numerous therapy techniques I have experienced, coupled with my discovery of Stoicism, have been instrumental in reshaping my approach to how I live my life and lead my company.

I have known for years that I had a book in me, but the timing never seemed as perfect as now. There is a dire need for authentic wellness and resilience strategies, particularly for people in high-stress professions. Too many first responder agencies across the country are desperate for solutions to mitigate the suicides and suffering within their ranks – and while this book focuses on leveling up your ability to understand human behavior and safely de-escalate volatile situations, it also offers insights and techniques that foster a thriving, resilient spirit.

Unarmed is a journey into the heart of what it means to thrive as a human beyond any profession, title, or rank. I want us to break down the barriers we erect in our minds and hearts that keep us disconnected from ourselves and separated from each other and open ourselves to the power of genuine human connection. As you dig into this book, you will find a blend of personal anecdotes, philosophical insights, and practical advice, all with the goal of evolving you toward a more courageous, compassionate, and connected way of living your life.

CHAPTER 1

Humanizing Crisis Management

"Men are disturbed not by things, but by the view
which they take of them." ~ Epictetus

When you think of de-escalation, what comes to mind? Many only consider it a policing term. While it has become more pervasive of late, de-escalation goes far beyond policing matters and is a skill every human being should have. Just as having a high emotional intelligence (EQ) is important, so is your ability to understand what de-escalation is and when it is needed. By the time you finish reading this book, you will have increased your competence and confidence when interacting with other people.

Everything changed for me when I realized the most useful weapon I would ever carry wasn't the one slung across my shoulder or on my hip. It was the one inside of me – my mind. It is our minds, individually and collectively. We have been taught most of our lives what to think or how to act, but we were never really taught how to think or leverage the superpower within us. This book will help you tap into that power. First, though, you must understand that the precursor for de-escalation is a person in crisis.

The Three Core Elements of a Crisis

The three core elements of a crisis are *Time*, an *Individual*, and what I call the *Environmental Stressor* or situation. Every crisis will have these three elements, and we have to be mindful not only of each one individually but also of how one changes depending on the other. Let's not only think about this externally, though, as if we never go into crisis ourselves. My preference is we should think about ourselves first. This is my first invitation to flipping norms on their head, a theme you will notice throughout this book. When we are doing what is required or best for ourselves, it allows everything else to fall into place much more easily.

Let's first accept that everything we believe is either because someone told it to us or we read it somewhere. But does that make it true, right, or the best way? It is just a way, and this is a great first step to recognizing human behavior as neutral instead of right and wrong. Take this book, for example. I'm not telling you to take everything I say as *the* way; rather, it is *one* way to handle situations more productively.

Now, to understand de-escalation, we must first understand what causes the need for it, and that is a crisis. A crisis is a temporary state of upset and disorganization characterized by the inability to cope with a particular situation using customary methods of problem-solving. So, what does this mean? As I mentioned, you must have those three components: person, time, and environmental stress.

What I tell people is we all have this God complex, and that's not a religious statement as much as it is this idea that we get to be the great deciders. When we believe that our way is the only way or the right way, we set ourselves up for failure. In fact, when I'm training or speaking to first responder groups, I tell them to imagine there is no such thing as right or wrong, good or bad. There just is. When we assume that there is good or bad, right or wrong, we create a disadvantage for ourselves. As Shakespeare writes in *Hamlet*, "There is nothing either good or bad, but thinking makes it so." This is important for us to understand, especially when it comes to knowing our minds.

Let's reflect on 9/11, a day that is deeply ingrained in our collective memory whether we were alive then or not. Each year, on its anniversary, we are reminded of what happened through videos, pictures, and memorial gatherings. One image that particularly stands out to me is the harrowing sight of people jumping from one of the towers. Why is this image so poignant? There was no way for firefighters to go up, and because the fire had fully engulfed the room, the people inside could not go down. Sadly, their only option to escape the flames was to jump from the building.

So, I pose this question to you. Let's call it a terrible version of the game "What would you do?" You're at work one day, minding your own business, and a plane crashes into the building. There's no way to go down, and nobody can come up and save you. This leaves you with two options: one, you can stay in the room and burn to death or maybe suffocate from smoke inhalation, or two, you can walk to the edge of your office building where the window has been smashed out and jump to your death. Which of these two horrible options would you choose? I want you to pause and really think about this.

Whatever your brain just decided, I know I would jump. But maybe, when the time came, I would never jump. Maybe I would stay in the room. The reality is that I have no idea what my actual response would be.

Understanding how we'll truly react in a given situation remains unknown until we face it. This uncertainty has long been a fundamental issue I've encountered with training methodologies. After over two decades of immersion in training environments, I've come to recognize a crucial truth: the human brain distinctly recognizes the difference between a training exercise and real-life scenarios. Despite the intensity of stress-inoculation drills, live-fire exercises, and tactical simulations in both military and policing contexts, there remains an inherent awareness that these are controlled, simulated environments.

My concern is in the realm of human behavior, where individuals who have never faced such high-stakes situations feel qualified to critique or analyze the actions of those who have. This disconnect creates a widespread challenge for organizations, both internally and externally.

Mike Tyson has a brilliantly astute quote: "Everybody has a plan until you get punched in the mouth." It's evident that in critical moments, we inevitably revert to our highest level of training. But we should not be so ignorant as to believe that just because someone completed a training, they will not make any mistakes. This reality underscores the complexity of preparing for real-world scenarios and the limitations of simulated training. Again, it's a reminder to see human behavior as neither right nor wrong.

Even when we have high-quality training, the unique stressors of any given environment invariably trigger a reaction within us. Our reactions are often a complex mystery, deeply rooted in our personal biases, upbringing, environment, and belief systems – elements that this book will explore and attempt to unravel.

Time

A critical concept I want to challenge here is our perception of time, particularly in crises. Time constraints are a human-constructed notion and irrelevant when it comes to de-escalating someone in distress. The urgency or pressure we feel due to such constraints can significantly influence our actions and decisions.

Consider a scenario where you're nearing the end of your shift, be it on the job or as you're winding down from a long day, and you're suddenly faced with an urgent matter – perhaps an email from your boss that demands immediate attention. The natural inclination to rush or even avoid dealing with the issue due to the impending end of your workday is a classic example of how time can impact our behavior. The resulting actions, whether it's neglecting the matter entirely or addressing it with less than your best effort, can lead to negative consequences. These could range from disciplinary actions to personal dissatisfaction, all stemming from our constructed urgency. Slowing down and thinking differently when managing these time-induced pressures can enhance our response quality in both personal and professional crises.

Many first responders can relate to this next dreaded scenario, one that's happened to me too many times. I'm at the end of a long shift, and due to things happening outside of work, I'm not just looking forward to getting off on time, but I am convinced I need to be off on time. And then, with 19 minutes left in my shift, there it is. The dispatcher calls my number. I key the radio and acknowledge, and she sends me clear across my district – or even worse, into someone else's district. *Freaking sandbagger,* I most likely think. And it is not an easy call, either; it is something horrible that will take a long time to handle.

Do we show up to encounters like this as our best selves? Do we lead with empathy and compassion? Do we have patience and kindness? Or, like me, do we feel offended in these moments, thinking, *How dare this person be in crisis right now? I have plans after work. I need to get my son to the dentist. Not only should this total stranger know I am busy with plans and about to get off my shift, but they should also care! The audacity.* Such scenarios are far too common, where the idea of "fairness" is activated, and we feel a disconnection from the person we are blaming for this situation.

We need to recognize that while time serves as a structured framework for our calendars and daily lives, it becomes irrelevant in the face of human crises. When someone is in a crisis, their behavior is not bound by the constraints of time. In fact, I can confidently say that one of the most effective approaches to handling a crisis is to deliberately slow down the perception of time, meaning, let's not stress tomorrow, next week, or even tonight. Instead, let's focus on the next five seconds and how we can survive this moment and make it to the next, not think about anything long-term right now.

Time is both your enemy and best friend, depending on which side you are on and how you use it. When I am confronted with someone in a crisis, and I know they need my help, I will take all the time I can. Later in this book, I'll share my experiences as a law enforcement officer in San Antonio, particularly with the mental health unit. I take great pride in a particular achievement from those years: for 11 years, I interacted with more than 8,400 individuals, many facing severe challenges like co-occurring disorders, substance abuse, and serious mental illnesses. Remarkably, I never once resorted to the use of force.

You might wonder, *How this was possible. Did luck play a role?* For sure, but was luck the only reason? Certainly not. There were times when using force would have been completely justified and even moments when my fellow officers would have supported such a course of action. Legally, I had the option to use force in certain situations to achieve the desired result. However, while using force would have satisfied my objectives, it wouldn't have led to a mutually beneficial outcome serving the interests of everyone involved.

The Individual

Now, let's look at the second element of a crisis: the individual. As with time, so much goes into this component, and we will dig deeper into the subject throughout the book. Who are you? Who are they? We're going to talk a lot about that in this book, but who you are is wherever you go, and wherever you go, there you are. We need to deepen our understanding of introspection across all aspects of our lives, whether in leadership, parenting, relationships, or as first responders.

In every role we play, the importance of self-reflection cannot be overstated. We must constantly ask ourselves, "Who am I, and what am I bringing into this current situation?" This awareness is crucial. If I'm not in the right headspace, if I'm running on little sleep, feeling hungry, or have just disagreed with my spouse or child, how will that affect my interactions with others facing their own challenges? It's essential to acknowledge the interplay between our personal issues and the situations we encounter. Although we often believe we can compartmentalize effectively, our emotions invariably influence our behaviors. These behaviors, in turn, either support our goals or create additional obstacles. Recognizing and managing this dynamic is key to navigating life's complexities effectively.

The Environmental Stressor

Finally, the third piece of a crisis is the environmental stressor. Recognize that the environment within a crisis is a dynamic entity, always fluid. Every situation, every moment, brings a change in the environment. Factors such as weather conditions, location, time of day, and lighting all contribute to this ever-changing landscape. These elements significantly influence how people behave and how you, as a responder, present yourself and act. A comprehensive understanding of these environmental stressors is crucial, especially in de-escalation scenarios.

Consider a situation where a single individual is in crisis. Flooding the scene with excessive personnel can often exacerbate the problem, not alleviate it. Personally, I've had a problem with how certain hostage negotiations are handled. Think of this as herd mentality. People will typically behave in a specific way when they are by themselves versus when they are around a group. This is in all aspects of behavior. Our emotions are exacerbated, positive or negative, when there is an audience. Think in terms of wavelengths and energy. If I am having a crisis and feeling sad, angry, frustrated, or agitated, and a group of four to six people surround me who are happy, excited, or even flat – it is possible I will become more of what I already am in that moment. It's also crucial to distinguish crises from critical incidents. A crisis tends to be personal, affecting an individual, whereas a critical incident might involve multiple people or even a natural disaster encompassing various simultaneous events.

Here's another situation I encountered numerous times as a police officer. Imagine a person threatening to jump off an overpass – they are suicidal. Ideally, the area should be secured by shutting off nearby traffic so the immediate vicinity can be controlled and isolated. This action not only safeguards the community, preventing potential further harm, like someone jumping into oncoming traffic, but also transforms the situation into a manageable, isolated incident. This approach underscores the importance of assessing and adapting to the environmental factors at play in every crisis scenario.

But here is what usually happens: all of these high-speed units show up with a lot of Kevlar and Velcro, 15 people deep, pointing long guns at a person who is contemplating ending their own life. I've never understood this. A lot of policies and protocols in many police departments simply do not make sense. I've always argued against this one in particular. My opinion isn't a popular one, but what I see is a person in crisis, not a reason to deploy all of our toys and rack up overtime pay.

Something else to consider when we look at a crisis is cultural context. We live in a culturally diverse society where trauma is universal. This cannot and should not be minimized or dismissed. We must be mindful of our biases, which should not deter us, especially when considering the breadth of cognitive biases identified in neuroscience research. Hundreds of different biases influence how we process information, think critically, and perceive our reality. This diversity in thought processes supports the idea that there are multiple paths to the same goal, which, in this context, is peace.

Moreover, it's essential to understand that different cultures have unique perspectives on the nature, cause, and management of behavioral health crises. The cultural context plays a significant role in how crises are perceived and handled. Acknowledging this diversity is crucial to effectively addressing and de-escalating situations involving individuals from various cultural backgrounds. Not all cultures view and respond to crises in the same way, and this diversity must be considered in our approaches.

The diversity of our world greatly enhances the richness of our global society. We must try to deepen our understanding of the myriad cultures around us, not just globally but also within our local neighborhoods. The variety in our communities brings with it distinct challenges and opportunities, aspects I have personally experienced and frequently addressed in the operations of police departments. And not always in a positive way.

A Little Bit About Myself

To share a bit of my background, I'm originally from New York. After joining the Marine Corps straight out of high school, I was stationed at Camp Pendleton in Southern California. Post-Marine Corps, at the suggestion of my best friend, Jesse, I moved to South Texas, specifically San Antonio, and immediately joined the police force.

My connection to Texas and San Antonio was entirely new, and I will admit I was geographically ignorant. I told Jesse he was ridiculous for thinking I would move to Texas. I truly believed the entire state was a farm. I am not a farmer. I am not a hunter. I am not anything I assumed Texas was. Of course, he laughed at me and assured me San Antonio was an actual city with highways and buildings. I could not believe it until I saw it.

As graduation from the police academy approached, we were asked to indicate our preferred work locations. San Antonio, like many major cities, boasts a diverse demographic, particularly in its inner-city areas. These neighborhoods are often vibrant and culturally rich, yet each presents unique challenges and dynamics. Typically, inner cities are predominantly populated by people of color. For instance, in San Antonio, the east side is largely African-American, while the south and west sides are mainly Hispanic. The north, northeast, and northwest sides present a more diverse mix of populations.

Eighteen years ago, during my time at the police academy, I received some stereotypical advice: "Hey, Joe, if you want to chase people, head to the east side, as the African-American community there tends to run from the police. If you're looking for physical confrontations and want to fight, the south or west side is where the Hispanic community tends to fight with us more. And if you prefer dealing with complaints or being complained about, the north side, being more affluent, has plenty of that."

I found that information odd. It seemed like an unusual statement to make, but what did I know? As a cadet in a police academy, I, along with many other enthusiastic individuals, was stepping into a profession that immersed us in inner-city communities with which we had no prior connection. My initial years were spent patrolling the south side of San Antonio, and I was largely unfamiliar with the Hispanic culture and language. Gradually, I learned and adapted, but it took me a year or two of daily interaction and experience to truly understand and connect with the community. This period was a significant learning curve, teaching me how to navigate and respect the cultural environment effectively.

I encourage everyone to take a moment to reflect and become more aware of how we perceive human tragedy, our personal feelings towards different people, ethnicities, colors, belief systems, and ideologies, something we probably do not do enough of. In the next chapter, we will discuss the concepts of in-groups and out-groups as understood in sociology. However, we need to recognize and understand our biases.

So, what was the key to my success during my tenure with the San Antonio Police Department? How did I manage over 8,400 human interactions without resorting to force? Sure, some might call it luck. At times, I was lucky. And yes, there were instances where using force would have been justified or even considered acceptable to achieve compliance or ensure safety. But early in my career, I adopted a mantra that I've adhered to ever since, both as a police officer and now as a business owner.

The mantra is simple yet profound: always focus on the person, not the problem. Put the individual first, the issue second. This approach is two-fold: prioritizing the person over the problem and understanding that establishing a connection is a prerequisite to making any correction. And yes, we do not want to sacrifice safety to build rapport – we can focus on people and still ensure scene safety.

For the parents reading this, the concept remains the same. Certainly, as a father, I understand there's an expectation that your children will listen to you. However, there's a significant difference between achieving voluntary compliance, a topic we'll explore, and merely eliciting compliance through fear. Similarly, for first responders, our communities mustn't respond to us from a place of fear. We should never desire to be feared, nor should we seek compliance through fear or intimidation. Instead, our goal should be to attain mutually beneficial outcomes by prioritizing the people involved.

I often advise first responder agencies to video record interviews with candidates, a practice already common in many police agencies. These interviews typically involve a panel asking the candidate why they want to become a police officer or join that specific agency. (I'd argue that all professions should video record their interviews). Then, every year, on the anniversary of their hiring, officers should revisit this recorded interview. It's a chance to reflect on who they were at that time and the thoughts and feelings they expressed.

I firmly believe that officers are genuinely sincere in their interviews. The challenge arises when they enter the training academy, where they encounter attempts to reshape their beliefs and perspectives and often develop fears and paranoia about the dangers of the world and the nature of people.

The issue with this is that many people will lose sight of their original motivations. When I speak to law enforcement groups, I remind them that if you feel frustrated by the problems of others, it's a sign that you've probably lost perspective on why you started. Remember, the problems of others are precisely what fuel your purpose. Whenever I encounter someone facing a challenge, it reinforces my role: I am here to serve, to assist others. Without this problem, what would I have to do? This book is a continuation of that mission from me to you. I aim to meet people where they are, helping them to focus not just on their problems but to feel acknowledged and understood first. Another key point is prioritizing connection over correction.

The CCRTC Model of De-Escalation

When it comes to helping people, first and foremost, it's important to establish a connection. To facilitate this, I've developed the CCRTC model of de-escalation, which stands for *Curiosity, Connection, Rapport, Trust,* and *Compliance.* Admittedly, it's not the most catchy or sleek acronym, but it encapsulates the essence of my policing career and the techniques that were key to my effectiveness in gaining compliance, even in challenging situations like convincing individuals to go to the hospital when they didn't want to or dealing with threats to my safety. And trust me, there were plenty.

Curiosity

The model begins with the first C: Curiosity. Curiosity serves as a counterbalance to judgment. For me, it is the antithesis of judgment. Often, without realizing it, we find ourselves quick to judge – judging others, ourselves, the world around us, and various situations. This tendency isn't entirely our fault; it's rooted in our evolutionary history. When our ancestors roamed the savannas with primitive minds, they were constantly on the lookout for threats. This instinct to identify danger has carried through to our modern cognition, often manifesting as judgment.

Our brains, despite evolving, still carry remnants of our ancestral past when survival meant scanning the savannas for threats. Today, we understand more about the brain than ever before, but its fundamental wiring remains – we are instinctively inclined to identify problems, threats, or potential harm. This is where the motivational triad comes in: seek pleasure, avoid pain, and conserve energy. The conservation of energy, particularly, is a primal instinct reserved for potential life-or-death scenarios.

So, what does curiosity entail in this context? It means focusing on the person rather than the problem and understanding that the problem can be a pathway to purpose. In every interaction, think of two bookends. The first bookend is curiosity, a key component of the CCRTC model. Curiosity means looking beyond the surface issue and asking the critical question: "What else could be true?" This isn't just about gathering more information; it's a strategy to pause and reflect rather than respond impulsively. By asking this question, we challenge ourselves to slow down, consider multiple perspectives, and respond with thoughtfulness instead of a mere habitual reaction.

Before you respond to an email, reply to a text, answer a phone call, step out of your car for a community response, or engage in any scenario, take a moment to ask yourself, *What else could be true?* This question is immensely powerful. It compels us to slow down our thoughts to question our usual patterns, our ingrained biases, and our preconceived notions about what we believe to be true. This pause creates a space for broader perspectives, allowing us to view the world through a wider lens rather than jumping to conclusions based on a narrow viewpoint.

Embracing curiosity naturally leads to forging connections. It's important to understand that connection is about reciprocity and building relationships. This concept can be challenging, especially for those in the first responder community. There's often a hesitation, a belief that maintaining strict professional boundaries means avoiding any personal connections with community members. Concerns about revealing personal details, like marital status or family information, are rooted in the fear of losing authority or being manipulated. However, this guarded approach can prevent meaningful interactions. Establishing genuine connections doesn't necessarily compromise professionalism or safety; instead, it can enhance mutual respect and understanding in relationships.

A key to my success as a police officer was harnessing the power of connection. It's about understanding the relationship, connecting energy with energy, sharing the same space, and interacting human to human. My focus has always been on the person, not just their problem. It's not that the problem is irrelevant, but it is usually a distraction from the core issue, which the person may not even be aware of. Without exception, every aspect of human behavior is a form of communication.

The issue at hand might be the reason for our interaction, granting me the authority to be present, whether as a police officer, a boss, or a leader. But once I am there, I recognize that the problem, as presented, is only a surface distraction. What truly matters is the person behind the problem. My best advice in these moments is to do what I call a "situational autopsy." By taking a step back and reviewing the last 72 hours or so, we often find the real roots of the behavior, which helps us understand and address the underlying issues more effectively.

Reflecting on the past three days can offer significant insight into somebody's current state. Consider their recent eating habits, sleep quality, home environment, and the people in their lives – both present and absent. Examine how they've been using their time. This introspection can reveal much about the underlying factors influencing any problematic behaviors they're experiencing at the moment.

Connection

Connection is fundamentally about relationships. Throughout my 15 years in policing, whenever community members asked me if I had ever been diagnosed with a mental illness or gone through a divorce, I always responded honestly – and I viewed my answer as an opportunity for them to see me as something other than my authority. However, it's noteworthy that no one ever asked for personal information like my mother's maiden name, Social

Security number, or home address – the kind of details that could lead to identity theft or other invasive actions.

In the CCRTC de-escalation model, connection is a pivotal component, emphasizing the transformative power of establishing genuine rapport between individuals, even within professional contexts where boundaries are essential. This principle holds profound significance for law enforcement professionals, asserting that police officers can, and indeed should, foster connections with the communities they serve. Such connections go beyond mere acquaintance, embodying a relationship founded on trust and respect.

It dismantles the notion of an impassable divide between officers and community members, advocating instead for a collaborative approach to safety and coexistence. By prioritizing connection, law enforcement (and anyone using these skills) can create a foundation for more effective de-escalation, where conflicts are managed and resolved through empathy, dialogue, and a shared commitment to the well-being of all involved. This approach not only enhances the efficacy of policing but also contributes to building a more cohesive, resilient community fabric.

Let's not view this possibility as a threat but rather a reminder. It's 2024, and in this digitally interconnected world, it's easier than ever for someone to find you or discover where you live. Our digital footprints make us more accessible than in the past. That's why it's crucial to find common ground when establishing connections with people. You'll often discover that you share more similarities than differences by intentionally focusing on the person in front of you. However, due to our evolutionary predispositions and a tendency to judge, we frequently fixate on the differences, overlooking our shared human experience.

For me, connection is one of the most glaring holes we face as a society. I created this model to help people understand their role, no matter their position, in fostering a more united community, organization, or household.

Human connection is a philosophy that champions the belief that every individual, no matter what they have done, deserves to be seen, valued, and offered love. It could be the one thing that helps them navigate the present hurdle they are facing.

Rapport

The next critical component of building effective relationships is rapport, an essential skill for fostering connections. Rapport is established through effective communication and active listening. While I won't cover rapport much in this chapter, please note the entirety of Chapter 3 is dedicated to this vital component of the de-escalation model.

Using the techniques in this book to establish rapport paves the way to building trust, which is the next component of the CCRTC model. I often say that trust involves some sort of a test. Before moving to the compliance phase, where I might need to ask someone to go to a hospital, be handcuffed, or enter a police car, establishing trust is key. How do we build this trust? It starts by not skipping the initial steps of leveraging curiosity, establishing a connection, and developing rapport.

Trust

To gain someone's trust, you should start with small tests. For example, if I can get someone to sit down, it demonstrates their willingness to comply, and it becomes more likely that they will agree to subsequent requests. It's crucial to acknowledge and thank them for their cooperation, reinforcing positive behavior. A simple "Hey, Jim, will you please have a seat for me?" or "Hey, Jim, would you mind sitting down with me?" can be more effective than a direct order. This approach of replacing orders with invitations is often the fastest way to gain compliance. For instance, rather than demanding, "Sit down," a more effective approach could be, "Would you join me in taking a seat?" This subtle shift can make a significant difference in establishing trust and gaining compliance.

Consider another scenario: perhaps the person you're interacting with is seated at a desk, holding an item like a pen, keychain, stuffed animal, or even a pill bottle. Approach them politely and ask, "Could I take a look at your pen, please?" Show genuine interest: "Wow, is this one of those gel pens that don't smear? I really like them. Oh, and it's a fine point – fantastic pen!" When you return it, make sure to express your gratitude: "Thank you so much for letting me take a look at this. I appreciate it."

Some might view this approach as manipulative, and to some extent, it is. But it's crucial to acknowledge that this is about understanding the dynamics of human behavior. The intent here isn't to manipulate for one's selfish gains but to create a situation that's beneficial for everyone involved. My goal is to use this understanding of human behavior not to exploit others but to achieve outcomes that are advantageous for them as well, especially when dealing with someone who has a serious mental illness and may not be aware of it.

Much of my experience has been with individuals who have mental health needs who often require additional guidance, reassurance, or encouragement regarding their safety. Once again, It's important for me that you understand the intent of this approach is not malicious. It's not about taking advantage of anyone or causing harm. Instead, it's about using the principles of human behavior to achieve voluntary compliance without resorting to force or intimidation.

Compliance

After establishing trust, even with a small action, the next step is to seek compliance, which often involves a more significant request. A critical point I emphasize, particularly for first responders, is the lack of training on how to proceed when someone says no to a lawful order. When faced with refusal, we're often left in a state of crisis, which I found myself unprepared for during my academy training. This gap in police academy training underscores the need for different approaches and strategies in these situations.

During my training in 2005, I was taught the "ATM" method: *Ask, Tell, Make.* The process starts with asking someone to do something. If they don't comply, you tell them more firmly. If they still don't comply, you "make" them do it, typically implying the use of force. This method often leads to rapid escalation, resorting to physical intervention or the use of equipment to enforce compliance, which tends to aggravate the situation further.

What we teach and encourage at SolutionPoint+ is a different approach to handling a no. When someone refuses to comply at the first attempt, I respond with a smile and tell myself, *They don't mean "no" forever, just "not now."* This refusal might indicate a lack of trust, insufficient rapport, or an absence of connection. It could also mean that I wasn't sufficiently curious at the onset of our interaction. Instead of starting from scratch, I reassess the situation by working backward through these steps. It's often a matter of being stuck at the trust stage.

I want you to imagine this process as descending a staircase. Each step represents a stage in building rapport and trust. When met with a no, it's not about going back to the top of the staircase; it's about stepping back to the last successful stage – often trust – and reassessing from there. This approach fosters a more thoughtful, patient, and effective method of reaching compliance.

Each goal achieved in this process is another step down a staircase, with compliance on the ground floor. If we reach the point of asking for compliance and they say no, it's a matter of taking one step back up to the trust level. If trust isn't the issue, then we return to active listening, a skill detailed in Chapter 3. This involves questioning whether we're asking the right questions and have successfully established rapport. If rapport is present but compliance is still lacking, there may be a connection issue.

By methodically working through these steps, we can often achieve our objectives. Please understand that while these techniques are effective in many situations, they are not foolproof. Guaranteeing a safe outcome every time would be an overstatement, considering the unpredictable nature of human behavior. There will always be exceptions – individuals who defy norms, resist the system, or refuse to comply. This is an expected part of working with people, and it's important to be prepared for such instances. With 11 years of experience working in the seventh-largest city in the country and after having more than 8,400 interactions without resorting to force, I can confidently say that these methods are effective.

The Core Principles for Achieving Compliance

As we conclude this chapter, I want to emphasize the core principles that are fundamental to understanding and achieving compliance as well as managing crises. It's crucial to recognize that behind every problem lies a person, and every problem is rooted in an emotion, which, in turn, stems from a thought. We will cover that in great detail later in the book.

The first step in any crisis or compliance situation is to become curious and then establish a connection before considering any form of correction. The CCRTC model is a valuable framework in this regard, and I encourage you to start practicing it in various aspects of your life. Practice it at home, in the workplace, during your next professional call, or even right now before you move to the next chapter. Challenge yourself, remain curious, and remember that curiosity is the direct opposite of judgment.

Every behavior is a form of communication, and our brains tend to find what they're looking for. This concept, known in psychology as confirmation bias and in spiritual circles as the law of attraction or manifestation, underscores the power of perspective. If you approach a problem while expecting a problem, that's likely what you'll find. However, you're more likely to foster a positive outcome if you approach it by seeking a solution and offering kindness and empathy.

You thought I was going to leave you hanging, didn't you? Let's address the back of the bookend, complementing the front I previously discussed. After every interaction, whether it's a call, a personal encounter, a work situation, a school issue, a PTA meeting, or an interaction with your children, remember to focus on the person, not the problem, and the vital role of curiosity. The back of the bookend is simply a form of a personal debriefing. Ask yourself, *What else could be true?* Then, at the conclusion, ask, *What role did I play in this outcome?*

This approach instills a sense of responsibility and prompts you to consider how your actions influenced the situation, which is necessary to learn and evolve along the way. If the outcome was positive, acknowledge your part in it. Recognize how effectively applying the CCRTC model led to de-escalation and compliance. It's not always about self-criticism; acknowledging your successes is equally important.

Conversely, when things don't go as planned, and this is especially true for my fellow officers, it's easy to fall into the trap of blaming the other party. A statement I've heard too many times is, "I had to [take this action] because they [did something]." But this mindset overlooks our own role in the situation.

It's a harsh truth that in many instances of the use of force in policing, the situation may have been escalated or provoked by the first responder. This isn't about assigning blame or inducing guilt. Many officers haven't received adequate training to effectively handle the realities of their communities. However, it's crucial to ask ourselves, "What did I do that might have contributed to the outcome not being as positive as it could have been? Did I invade their personal space, raise my voice, or act hastily?" These are learning opportunities, moments to reflect on our actions and their impacts and understand how we might inadvertently contribute to less-than-ideal outcomes.

CHAPTER 2

Challenge Your B.S.

"Everything we hear is an opinion, not a fact. Everything we see is a perspective, not the truth." ~ Marcus Aurelius

Have you ever experienced a moment when you were certain about a decision, only to be met with skepticism or doubt by someone close to you? That happened to me when I decided to join the Marine Corps straight out of high school. Why the Marines? Well, my father was in the U.S. Navy when I was born, and clearly, I could not follow in his footsteps.

Originally, I had planned to go to college and pursue my passion for soccer, but life took a different turn when I became a father in my senior year. A Marine Corps recruiter who was aware of my situation visited our school. He was persuasive, presenting the Marines as a solution to my newfound responsibilities and assuring me the Marines would take care of everything for my daughter and me. When I mentioned my interest in soccer, he cleverly noted that the Marine Corps had a soccer team, which piqued my interest. In hindsight, at 17 years old, a new dad, and quite naive, the idea of playing soccer for the Marine Corps seemed like a dream opportunity. Okay, okay, I was dumb AF.

How many military veterans are laughing at me at this point, thinking, *Yeah, right, no one joins the Marine Corps to play soccer?* Well, this recruiter was talking to a 17-year-old kid who knew nothing about anything and got him excited, thinking he could play soccer for the Marine Corps. He did advise me that I needed a job. I had no idea what I wanted to do, so I told him I just wanted something easy. He asked me if I wanted to deploy, and I said no. He asked me if I wanted to be stationed close to home in the northeast, and I said yes. So, he signed me up for some "easy" job. I go to my training school in Camp Lejeune, realizing I'm going to be working in finance and supply, only to then learn that I'm stationed in Southern California in an infantry unit.

This story does have a silver lining, though. As it turned out, my recruiter didn't exactly deceive me. I did get to play soccer in the Marine Corps – just once, in Iraq, against some incredibly skilled, shoeless children. Had he been upfront and told me my sole soccer experience in the Marines would be a game in Iraq post-9/11, I doubt I would have had the courage to enlist. Contrary to some combat veterans who speak of war with pride and patriotism, I won't glorify the experience of conflict and taking a life. The truth is, it shattered me. I broke the first time I pulled the trigger of my government-issued M-16 and saw another human drop dead.

Now, rewinding to my early days in Marine Corps boot camp, there's a practice in the military where you're issued dog tags. These tags include your last name, the last four digits of your Social Security number, your blood type, gas mask size, and religious preference. Every Marine receives these. When it was my turn, I stated "no preference" for my religious belief. This was a personal choice shaped by various factors in my life.

When I returned home on leave, my father, a Navy veteran, saw my dog tags and was taken aback. "What the hell is this?" he asked. Confused, I thought he was questioning the tag itself. I explained, somewhat naively, that it was the religious preference section. He knew that, but he was perplexed as to why I had chosen "no preference." "Your grandmother would roll in her grave if she knew you put no preference," he said. His reaction left me reflecting on the complex interplay of personal beliefs, family expectations, and identity.

He told me, "Joe, you're Catholic." I was completely shocked. I couldn't recall ever setting foot in a church, nor did I remember participating in any church-related activities during my childhood. Yet, according to my father – and confirmed later by my grandmother – I was Catholic. So, upon returning to my duty station, I requested an update to my dog tags to reflect my newfound Catholic identity.

My story took another turn when my time in the Marine Corps came to a close, and I was about to receive my honorable discharge. A few of us decided to get what is known as "meat tags," tattoos of our dog tags on our rib cages, so now I permanently carry a tattoo declaring my Catholic faith, a faith I still know very little about and would declare I have nothing to do with.

This anecdote illustrates the peculiarities of belief systems and how they are often handed down to us. Our beliefs can be much like hand-me-down clothes, which may not fit perfectly or be stained or worn. We receive them not by choice but as a legacy from those before us, and we are often expected to wear them with pride and gratitude regardless of whether they truly resonate with our personal experiences or understanding. Essentially, we are wearing someone else's identity.

This is very similar to how we adopt our beliefs, values, ethos, and perceptions of the world. And because we develop this habit so early on, we blindly follow a path that was never really meant for us. To me, that is where so much of the anxiety and depression of today comes from. And no, as a mental health advocate, I am not minimizing the science or complexities of any mental illness, nor would I ever.

A perspective I hold, which may not be widely popular, is that our public education system has inadvertently become a feeder for the mental and behavioral health systems. The reason? The lack of sufficient curriculum options to cater to diverse learning styles. Students are often groomed for standardized tests rather than equipped with skills for real-world challenges.

While I have harbored this thought for over a decade, I was recently recommended a book by a friend of mine who is "unschooling" her children, a concept with which I was not familiar. The book *Dumbing Us Down* by John Taylor Gatto resonated with me not because it validated my opinion but because it provided real-life context from a New York City teacher with over 30 years of experience. Schools are treated as businesses where kids are merely numbers, getting lost in the machinery. They are not taught how to live a quality life but rather to follow orders and seek permission or approval for everything they do.

One excerpt from the book reads, "If we face the present school and community crisis squarely, with hopes of finding a better way, we need to accept that schools, as networks, create a large part of the agony of modern life. We don't need more schooling; we need less." While this book is not solely about that one issue, I am fascinated by how the problem I am trying to solve – eradicating suicide – becomes exacerbated. Government-created and -controlled schools with misaligned curricula detach young people from their highest potential.

Have you ever played that hypothetical game where you imagined what you would do if you were in charge for a day? What rules would you implement? What laws would you change? What would you do to improve your community, society, or even the world if given absolute authority for just one day? I find myself engaging in this thought experiment quite frequently. As you'll discover throughout this book, one of the many changes I would advocate for is a complete overhaul of our public education system.

The idea of challenging our B.S. – belief system – should begin at an early age. I have observed numerous young adults who are frustrated, directionless, and overly critical of themselves. Why is this the case? I believe it's largely due to societal expectations tied to age-related milestones. There's an unspoken rule that by 18, you should be heading to college; by your early to mid-twenties, you should be graduating, and shortly after that, you should be embarking on a career. By your late twenties, the expectation is to settle down, find a partner, purchase a house, and start a family.

This sequence, which I refer to as the "American order of operations" – finish high school, go to college, secure a job, marry, buy a house, have children, work until retirement, and then eventually pass away – is often seen as the blueprint for the American dream. But how many have followed this path only to find themselves questioning their choices? They wonder why they pursued a particular degree that they're no longer passionate about, why they're stuck in a job they don't enjoy, why they're with a partner they're not sure about, why they live in a town that doesn't feel like home, or why they're playing it safe when they have a burning desire to achieve and be more. I often had this feeling in my own life, like I was in the passenger seat, just watching life happen to me. Then, I decided to step off the hamster wheel and into the driver's seat.

While I wouldn't advise anyone to become a parent in their teens as I did, having my daughter during my senior year of high school was a pivotal moment that shaped my future. Without her, I often think I would have remained in Upstate New York, living a life that didn't align with my aspirations – perhaps working in a factory or a similar job (thanks, Axel). Not that there's anything inherently wrong with those jobs – they are essential and respectable – but they weren't for me. The truth is, back then, I had no clear idea of who I wanted to become. Now, at 42, I can honestly say that my journey of self-discovery didn't truly begin until I was around 37.

It's a common misconception among young adults – those who are 17, 18, or in their early 20s – that they should have their lives figured out, know their passions, and understand what they should be striving towards. But why this rush? This very pressure plants the seeds of the compulsion to please others. Many people live their lives trying to meet the expectations of their family, community, school, or friends rather than following their own paths.

What if we all truly took charge of our lives? What if we exercised our free will without concern for others' opinions or judgments? I have met numerous individuals who, burdened with this kind of dissatisfaction and depression, doubt their ability to endure until retirement. It's a profound realization that our choices and the pressures we succumb to profoundly affect our sense of fulfillment and happiness.

While I was with the San Antonio Police Department, teaching wellness classes during in-service training, I frequently encountered officers who approached me with deep concerns. They would confide in me, saying things like, "Joe, I don't think I can make it to retirement," or "I'm not sure I can keep doing this job." Initially, I assumed they were nearing retirement, only to be surprised when they revealed they had just started, were only a year in, or still had as many as 17 years left. In first responder circles, there's often a tendency to scoff at such sentiments, to ridicule officers who express doubts about their ability to continue in the role for the long haul.

Instead of mocking or dismissing these officers, we should encourage and support them. It takes significant courage and self-awareness for someone to realize that this line of work might not be the right fit for them. These individuals went through the rigorous process of background checks, fitness tests, police academy training, and actual fieldwork, only to discover that the reality of the job didn't align with their expectations or desires. Acknowledging this and choosing to pursue a different path requires bravery and should be commended.

I always encouraged these officers to trust their instincts if they felt the job wasn't right for them while also advising them to make responsible decisions, especially if they had families to consider. In such situations, the guidance of an advisor, mentor, therapist, or coach can be invaluable. I speak from experience. When I left the San Antonio Police Department after 15 years, the criticism and ridicule I faced for that decision were unbelievable. Other officers could not believe I was leaving the career just five years shy of having a pension – "for the rest of my life." But I knew I was done. So why stay in a place you no longer love, have passion for, or feel wanted?

When my time came to leave the Marine Corps after fulfilling my four-year contract, my departure was met with understanding and respect. No one shamed or challenged me, nor did anyone call me foolish or unwise. Instead, I was celebrated, thanked, appreciated, and then simply allowed to move on.

This experience leads me to another viewpoint I hold: in law enforcement, perhaps we should consider implementing contract-based tenures. A five-year contract would offer leverage and clarity to both the agency and the officer. After five years, there would be an opportunity for mutual evaluation. Maybe the officer isn't the right fit for the agency, or perhaps they are an exceptional first responder who could negotiate better working conditions, new days off, or a chance at a specialty unit. All too often, we just accept the status quo, much like those hand-me-down clothes we inherit without question. This topic, along with the concepts of wellness and resiliency, is covered more fully in Chapter Eight, particularly fixed versus growth mindset.

Two pivotal factors have significantly influenced my life for the better: therapy and the discovery of Stoicism. Both required me to unlearn much of what I knew and embrace new learning. Discovering authors like Ryan Holiday, a leading expert in Stoic philosophy, was a turning point for me. His work resonated with me, making me feel seen and empowered, inspiring me to reframe my entire perspective.

Imagine your mind is like an old city or town. Moving to a new city involves a steep learning curve – navigating traffic, finding restaurants, entertainment spots, and more. It's a rapid process of discovery, during which many opinions and ideas about how things could or should begin to form. This analogy reflects how we can approach reshaping our beliefs and understanding of the world around us.

Now, picture this: a year after moving to the city, you're not only given the proverbial keys to the city but also appointed city planner and endowed with a limitless budget and resources. What changes would you implement? Which aspects would you preserve? What would you enhance? And what would you demolish to make room for new, improved structures? This scenario mirrors the power we possess over our minds. You have the authority to be the mastermind of your mental landscape. What aspects of your thinking no longer serve you and need to be dismantled? Which elements are functioning well and should remain untouched?

Let's extend this analogy. Imagine you're at work, and your boss walks in, radiating enthusiasm, and announces that you're receiving a brand-new laptop to acknowledge your valuable contribution to the organization. Overwhelmed with pride and excitement, you unbox this new gadget, savoring the removal of the stickers and screen protector. You power it up, only to discover it's running an obsolete operating system, like Windows 96 or Mac OS 10 Cheetah from 2001. Your initial excitement fades to disappointment. Despite its newness, the laptop is practically useless with such an outdated system, unable to support current software.

This situation is akin to how we often operate our minds. How many of us are functioning on an equivalent of MS-DOS in our thought processes? Are we stuck with outdated perceptions and beliefs like an old Cheetah OS? Just as we regularly update our technology, we need to continually upgrade our thinking and belief systems. When our phones or computers prompt an update, we usually do it without a second thought. But what prompts us to update our mindset?

I want to emphasize that this isn't about merely rearranging the existing pieces in your life, hoping for satisfaction or joy. Changing your partner, relocating, switching jobs, buying new things, or planning vacations – these are superficial alterations. They don't guarantee improvement or happiness because the common denominator in all situations is *you*. True change comes from within, not just from altering external circumstances.

As you work your way through this book, I invite you to engage in an ongoing dialogue with yourself. With each question I present, I encourage you not just to read and move on but to pause and really think through your responses. Consider journaling your thoughts – it's a powerful way to process and reflect. You might even feel compelled to share your insights with me, fostering a deeper connection through our shared journey of self-exploration.

It's important to recognize that challenging your belief system, your B.S., is not simply about the pursuit of happiness. Happiness, as we often experience it, is fleeting, heavily influenced by our current circumstances or "happenings." This realization is profound, but what if we could discover something more enduring, like true joy? Joy is a state that remains steadfast even when life presents challenges. Unlike happiness, which ebbs and flows, joy persists. It arises from being in alignment with our true selves, free from the fear of judgment or ridicule.

Reflect on the changes you've implemented in your life over the past year. How have they contributed to the "city planning" of your mind? Have they brought you closer to who you truly want to be? And what about the immediate future? Acknowledge the steps you can take today, however small, that will bring you nearer to your goals.

As we prepare to transition into the next skill-based chapter, focusing on effective communication and active listening, it's crucial to understand that your prowess in communication is intrinsically linked to your ability to understand yourself. Engaging in introspection, challenging your existing belief systems, and upgrading your mental "operating system" are essential steps in this journey.

These processes are more than self-improvement tactics; they are fundamental to realizing your full potential as a communicator and, ultimately, as a person. In the next chapter, we will explore how enhancing your communication skills can profoundly impact your personal and professional life, illustrating the undeniable connection between self-awareness and effective interaction with others.

CHAPTER 3

Gimme That Pie

"Silence is better than unmeaning words."

~ Epictetus

Free Offer

T he ability to communicate with confidence and competence is invaluable for achieving fulfillment and success in your personal and professional life. This chapter is dedicated to the R in the CCRTC model, which stands for "Rapport." Effective communication and active listening are central to establishing rapport. In my experience, these skills are akin to a superpower, significantly enhancing your ability to succeed in various aspects of life.

For the 11 years I worked in the mental health unit of a major city's police department, I never had to resort to force. I attribute this accomplishment to my profound understanding of these communication skills. My career has included numerous training sessions in communication, hostage negotiation, and crisis negotiation. The essence of what I've learned and practiced boils down to a fundamental framework, which I will explain in detail in this chapter.

I want to assure you that the skills of effective communication and active listening are learnable. Regardless of whether you're a beginner or have undergone training, we all possess certain habits that can be improved. As someone who considers themselves an expert in these skills, I can attest that perfection is not always achievable, and that's okay. Patience with yourself is key – mastering these skills won't happen overnight. It generally takes about 18 months of consistent practice and application to truly master them, after which they become almost second nature. The key to remember while you fine-tune your skills is how important empathy is. Even if you make a mistake, people will be more accepting of you if you have genuine empathy.

Communication is a critical element in every sphere of life, whether business, leadership, parenting, relationships, sales, policing, or anything else. Surprisingly, most of us have never been formally taught how to communicate effectively. Being an effective communicator means being a better listener, and that's what we will explore and develop throughout this chapter.

We must accept that how we communicate with other people can either escalate or de-escalate a situation. As I alluded to at the end of Chapter 1, instead of simply saying, "I had to [take this action] because they [did something]," we should take ownership and responsibility. The impact of communication in every situation cannot be overstated. Acknowledging that not every problem can be attributed to others is vital.

An opinion of mine that often meets resistance among police officers is that approximately 50% of the time when an officer uses force, the responsibility lies with the officer rather than the citizen. The officer escalates the situation, often without malice or awareness of doing so. How can I make such a claim? My perspective is informed by extensive experience in a large police department and my time on the Chief's Action Advisory Board, where I was exposed to a wide array of scenarios.

I don't mean to indiscriminately place blame on first responders. The real issue often lies in the lack of appropriate training. Why should we expect first responders to always handle situations correctly if they haven't been adequately trained for the diverse challenges they face? Such an expectation seems both unreasonable and unfair.

Consider this analogy. You're at a quick-service oil-change facility, sitting in your car while the service is performed. Suddenly, your spouse or friend begins to choke on a piece of candy. In a panic, you call for help. A vehicle technician, acting with good intentions, attempts a version of the Heimlich maneuver. Unfortunately, their efforts are unsuccessful, and tragically, your friend doesn't make it. Would it be reasonable to blame the mechanic for not saving your friend? Clearly, the answer is no.

Expecting a mechanic to be CPR-certified or a medical expert seems far-fetched, yet we often place similar expectations on law enforcement officers. We demand they be experts in all societal issues and faultless in their responses despite the fact that their training may not cover the breadth of situations they encounter daily. This disconnect highlights the need for a more realistic understanding and approach to the skills and training required in law enforcement and first responder roles.

Understanding the distinction between hearing and listening is crucial, particularly in today's world, where we are bombarded with distractions from the moment we wake up until we go to sleep. It's important to realize that the average adult's attention span is now only about 8.25 seconds. As you read this book, think about how often you've become distracted or found your mind wandering. Our propensity for multitasking has impaired our ability to concentrate on anything for a prolonged period. This is where I am hoping to help you. Before breaking down the specific skills for effective communication and active listening, let's explore some of their foundational principles.

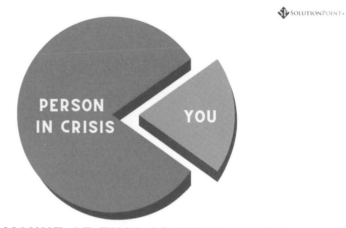

AMOUNT OF TIME SPENT TALKING

The first principle to understand is the "golden rule" of communication, commonly known as the 80-20 rule. This rule suggests that in a situation where someone is in crisis, we should allow them to do 80% of the talking while we speak only 20% of the time. If you find yourself speaking more than half of the time, you are likely attempting to dominate, control, or force an outcome that may not align with what the person in crisis desires or needs. Sometimes, the most effective approach is to step back, truly listen, and pay attention not just to what is being said but also to what remains unsaid. This concept is based on the 7/38/55 theory of communication by Dr. Albert Mehrabian, Professor Emeritus of Psychology at UCLA, known for his work on the importance of verbal and nonverbal messages.

To understand Dr. Mehrabian's theory, imagine a "communication pie" with three slices, each representing different aspects of communication: content (the actual words spoken), voice intonation (tone, volume, and pace), and body language (eye contact and physical movements). What percentage of this pie would you attribute to content? Many people guess figures like 50%, 20%, or 15%, but surprisingly, the answer is just 7%. Meaning, only 7% of the pie is made up of content (words spoken), whereas 38% is tone, and 55% is body language. See graph below.

When visualized on a graph, you can appreciate how small this 7% is. Personally, as a fan of a good Dutch apple pie, I would be offended if you only gave me a 7% slice. This demonstrates that while the words we say matter, they have significantly less impact than the tone of our voice and our body language. Despite this, many people react strongly to words alone. Understanding this distribution should encourage us to focus more on how we say things and our non-verbal cues, which are often more influential than the words themselves.

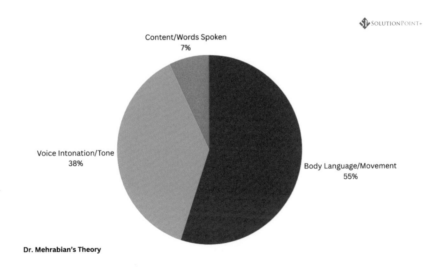

MOREPIE

As we cover the seven skills of effective communication and active listening, there's a helpful acronym to help you remember them: MOREPIE. This acronym represents a simplified approach to communication skills that I've found extremely effective. Despite the myriad of training programs and variations out there, from the FBI's version to the advanced and basic levels of hostage/crisis negotiation training, they all boil down to the same concepts.

The goal here is to distill the essence of effective communication into manageable parts. The seven skills we will focus on are:

- **Minimal encouragement**
- **Open-ended questions**
- **Reflective mirroring**
- **Emotional labeling**
- **Paraphrasing**
- **I-messages**
- **Effective pausing**

MOREPIE. Each letter in the acronym represents a skill, and mastering them can significantly enhance your communication in various situations. Some courses add an "S" at the end for "summarizing" or forming MOREPIES, but to me, summarizing and paraphrasing are too similar, and I am all for making things as easy as possible.

I'll explain each skill in the order I teach them – how we will most likely use them.

Emotional Labeling

Let's start with emotional labeling, which is often the first skill to be used in any interaction, particularly those that are face-to-face. A common question is whether you can use emotional labeling if the other person hasn't spoken yet. The answer is yes. Thanks to Dr. Mehrabian's theory, we know that a significant portion of communication is non-verbal.

It's also important to remember that emotional labeling is based on observation, not assumption. We never tell someone what they are feeling;

rather, we express our thoughts as observations or opinions. The formula is simple: "You look..." "You sound..." or "You seem..." For example, "You look frustrated," or "You seem upset," or "You sound annoyed."

It's important not to overlap these skills, except for effective pauses, which should follow each skill application. If you apply a skill and then pause, but there's no immediate response, resist the urge to fill the silence. Allow the pause to linger, even if it extends for 30 seconds or two minutes. The objective of the effective pause is to provide space for the other person to process their thoughts and respond when they feel ready.

The purpose of an emotional label is to connect with the person's emotional state rather than just react to their words. Remember, when someone is agitated, yelling, or even making threats, as the principle of 7% reminds us, the actual words form a minor part of the overall communication. What's more crucial is recognizing and responding to the emotional undercurrents of the interaction.

When someone appears angry, the focus should be on their emotional state, not the specifics of what they're articulating. People often use behaviors as a means to express emotions they cannot articulate, particularly in a world where EQ is not universally high. There's a prevalent notion, especially among men, that anger is the mask of depression. Many men report growing up with the understanding that only two emotions were socially acceptable: anger and happiness. Consequently, if an adult male feels scared, sad, overwhelmed, or stressed – emotions not associated with happiness – they often manifest as anger. The problem is we tend to get sidetracked by people's behaviors or the words they say instead of focusing on the underlying emotions driving those behaviors.

The next time you encounter someone who seems angry, consider the possibility that there may be underlying sadness, stress, worry, fear, or overwhelm. They might lack the skill to say, "I am feeling scared right now," and instead find it easier to express anger and project blame outward. This issue is prevalent not just in community settings but also in family and work environments. We should look beyond people's words to find the root cause of their emotions, as emotions are the true drivers of behavior.

The Effective Pause

The next skill is the Effective Pause, which leverages people's discomfort with silence. As effective communicators, whether we are interventionists, active listeners, family members, parents, spouses, or leaders, we must recognize that most people aren't trained to handle silence. Embracing this silence can be a powerful tool in communication, allowing space for processing and reflection for ourselves and the person we are engaging with. This skill, when mastered, can transform interactions, making them more meaningful and insightful.

Mastering the art of silence is an invaluable skill, especially considering that most people find silence uncomfortable. Silence is not just a lack of noise; it's a powerful communication tool that can be leveraged in various contexts, whether you're an interrogator, an investigator, a parent dealing with a teenager, or in any situation that calls for eliciting more information.

When combined with the other skills in the MOREPIE framework, silence can be particularly effective. It often leads to confessions, admissions, or the sharing of information that individuals might not have intended to reveal. The power of the pause lies not only in its use as a punctuation mark at the end of each communication skill but also in its inherent ability to prompt further dialogue.

Silence creates a void that people feel the need to fill, often leading them to divulge more than they planned. However, the untrained individual might find silence unsettling and may feel compelled to break it by speaking or deflecting, thus losing the opportunity silence provides. The key to leveraging silence effectively is patience – waiting for the other person's response, even if it takes minutes. Eye contact plays a crucial role during these moments. It's important to maintain a steady, non-threatening gaze, not to intimidate but to convey attentiveness and engagement.

In situations where the other person becomes agitated or confronts you about the silence, saying things like, "Why are you just staring at me?" It's crucial to maintain composure and calmly explain your intentions. Acknowledge their discomfort without matching their tone. Speak in a way that is low and slow, clear and brief, regardless of the other person's emotional state. This approach applies whether the person is highly agitated or speaking in a barely audible whisper. Your delivery should remain calm, slow, clear, and brief. This consistency in your communication style demonstrates control, understanding, and a non-threatening stance, essential elements in effective communication and active listening.

Open-Ended Questions

The skill of asking open-ended questions is crucial to effective communication and active listening. Open-ended questions elicit more than a simple yes or no response. They invite a fuller, more descriptive answer, encouraging the person to open up and share more information. Many people, however, fall into the habit of asking closed questions that start with phrases like "Have you," "Will you," "Do you," "Are you," or "Can you." These typically result in one-word answers and are not conducive to fostering open dialogue. If you find yourself receiving brief responses, reflect on the type of questions you're asking and adjust your approach.

When your goal is to encourage someone to share, and you find yourself receiving minimal responses, recognize that the responsibility lies with you, the conversation initiator, to pose better, more open-ended questions. While there are contexts, such as in a suicide assessment, where closed questions may be strategically used, open-ended questions are generally more effective. They are particularly valuable when you have limited time with someone and need to maximize the conversation's depth and breadth. These questions align with the 80-20 golden rule, allowing the other person to do most of the talking while you listen and gather insights.

A simple technique to encourage open-ended responses is to start your questions with "Tell me," for instance, "Tell me about your day," "Tell me what happened when…" "Tell me what you would like to see happen," or "Tell me what's been going on." These prompts naturally lead to more detailed responses.

Interestingly, this approach aligns with insights from various fields, including medicine. For instance, we were providing training at the Federal Bureau of Prisons, and an M.D. who participated in a de-escalation course we created shared that in medical training, they were taught that one good open-ended question could yield more information than a lengthy checklist of closed questions. This approach is supported by research indicating that when patients are given around four minutes to speak uninterrupted, they tend to reveal more pertinent information than they might in response to a series of specific queries, more proof of how universal these skills truly are.

The key to leveraging open-ended questions effectively is to ask one question at a time. This helps maintain clarity and focus, allowing the person you're engaging with to fully address each question without feeling overwhelmed or confused. Remember, the goal is to create space for the other person to express themselves, often leading them to share more than they initially planned. This approach can be transformative in building rapport and understanding, whether in personal relationships, professional settings, or crisis interventions.

We need to be wary of the rapid-fire approach when asking questions, especially in situations involving high stress or crisis. It's not uncommon for individuals, particularly those new to the practice of active listening, to barrage others with questions. This usually happens when they're nervous or unsure. Their thoughts race, leading them to jump from one question to another without waiting for a response. They might start with one question, but as their minds race, they pivot to another and then another, often ending up asking several questions in quick succession before pausing for a reply.

This approach can be counterproductive, especially when dealing with someone in an acute crisis. Bombarding people with multiple questions can exacerbate their stress and anxiety, potentially escalating the situation rather than calming it. To avoid this, it's important to consciously slow down your thought process and verbal delivery. Remember, your goal is to facilitate a calm, productive dialogue, not to overwhelm the person you're communicating with.

A useful technique is to focus on framing one well-thought-out question at a time, prefacing it with "Tell me." This encourages more detailed responses and stories and helps keep the conversation focused and meaningful. After posing your question, employ the effective pause – a deliberate silence that allows the other person time to process the question and formulate their response. This practice not only demonstrates respect for the person's thoughts and feelings but also fosters a more thoughtful conversation.

By asking one good question at a time, followed by a pause, you create an environment conducive to open communication. This allows the person you're engaging with to fully express themselves without feeling rushed or overwhelmed. It's a simple yet powerful way to enhance a connection and build rapport, whether in personal relationships, professional interactions, or during critical interventions.

Paraphrasing

The next skill is paraphrasing, or distilling a wide array of information into its essential elements. This technique is crucial for effective communication. Visualize a funnel with a wide top and narrow bottom. When someone pours their thoughts, feelings, and experiences into a conversation – much like pouring liquid into the mouth of a funnel – it can be overwhelming. A good communicator, like a skilled therapist, functions as the narrow end of the funnel, sifting through this deluge of information to identify and articulate the core elements of what's been said.

The art of paraphrasing is not about repeating everything verbatim. Instead, the idea is to capture the essence of the speaker's message. It involves actively listening to the person's venting – which, by the way, is a crucial process in itself. When someone needs to vent, it's important to allow them the space to do so without interruption. Venting can be a powerful way for people to process emotions and experiences, and the listener needs to acknowledge and validate these feelings.

Paraphrasing means summarizing the key points of what has been shared. Achieving this is straightforward: "So, what I'm hearing you say is…" followed by a few bullet points that encapsulate the primary themes or issues raised. My advice is to never use more than three bullet points. This shows the speaker that you're actively engaged and helps focus the conversation on the most pertinent issues. If you get a detail wrong and the speaker corrects you, that, too, has multiple benefits. Beyond clarifying the content, it shifts the power dynamic back to them, keeping them at ease.

Remember, the goal is not to regurgitate an exhaustive list of details but to distill the conversation into its most significant parts. This condensation helps both the speaker and the listener gain a clearer understanding of the main concerns at hand, facilitating a more focused and effective dialogue. By employing paraphrasing, you demonstrate active listening and guide the conversation toward meaningful insights and resolutions.

For example, imagine you have a friend, Eric. One day, he comes into work visibly upset, and you ask, "Hey, Eric, what's going on?" He starts venting about his current challenges: his wife's job loss during COVID-19, her reluctance to return to work, his increased workload to compensate for the lost income, and the resulting strain on their relationship and family life.

After listening to his outpouring of frustration, you can paraphrase what you've heard to show you're actively engaged and understand his predicament: "Wow, Eric, it seems like ever since your wife got laid off, things have been really tough at home." This isn't about dismissing the other details Eric shared but focusing on the core issue he's facing. It's a tool for clarification and ensuring accurate understanding.

If Eric corrects you, saying the real issue is the overtime he's working and his wife's reaction to it, embrace this as part of the process. Paraphrasing is about creating a space for such clarifications, enhancing the dialogue's precision. Remember, the goal of active listening isn't to fix problems but to understand and connect. Too often, particularly in close relationships, we rush to offer solutions when our partners might be seeking empathy and understanding.

Here's a tip I learned in marital therapy. Before jumping into problem-solving mode, ask your partner or the person you're conversing with what they need at that moment: "Do you need advice, or do you need me to just listen right now?" This simple question can prevent misunderstandings and help you provide the support they actually need.

Paraphrasing isn't just repeating words; it's capturing the essence of the conversation and feeding it back in a concise manner. Saying, "So, what I'm hearing you say is…" followed by no more than three key points ensures that you stay on track and respectful of the speaker's message. This approach not only validates the speaker's feelings but also encourages further exploration of the underlying issues, paving the way for a deeper connection.

Minimal Encouragement

Minimal encouragement is a subtle yet powerful active listening skill in which you use brief phrases or sounds to show you're engaged in the conversation without interrupting the speaker's flow. You guide the conversation, nudging the speaker to continue sharing their thoughts and feelings without completely taking over its direction.

Picture this: You're on a phone call. There are two types of callers: those who need minimal encouragement and those who don't. Take my mother, for example. She can embark on a storytelling marathon without any cues from me. I could set the phone aside, and she'd still weave her tale, completely unfazed by my silence. On the other hand, some callers need frequent acknowledgment to feel heard. Soon after they start talking, they pause and ask, "Are you still there?" seeking minimal encouragement to continue.

This skill isn't about dominating the conversation; it's about facilitating it. Using simple utterances like "uh-huh," "mm-hmm," "wow," "oh," "yeah," "sure," "hmm," "ah," "interesting," "really," or "okay" can effectively convey your presence and attentiveness. These small acknowledgments signal to the speaker that you're actively listening, encouraging them to delve deeper into their narrative.

Minimal encouragement is like gently tugging on a loose thread on one of your favorite shirts. You expect a small piece to come away, but instead, the thread keeps unraveling, revealing more and more of the fabric's story. However, while the technique is generally helpful, it's essential to use it judiciously. Overdoing it or using it inappropriately can disrupt the speaker's train of thought or make the conversation feel forced and unnatural.

The key is to be attuned to the speaker's rhythm and respond accordingly. For people who thrive on these subtle cues, your minimal inputs can help unravel the layers of their story, providing a richer, more comprehensive understanding. For those who require less, a sensitive and discerning approach ensures you're providing just enough engagement to keep the conversation meaningful and connected.

The art of minimal encouragement is nuanced, and even commonly used responses like "okay" require thoughtful consideration. While "okay" can serve as a form of minimal encouragement, it may not always be the most effective choice. In fact, my suggestion is to just get rid of it altogether. The challenge is to be more intentional with your responses to truly reflect active listening.

Consider the subtle implications of using "okay" during a conversation. It's a familiar, almost automatic response, but it can sometimes signal passive agreement or even indifference. Imagine a scenario where someone shares a detailed account or expresses deep emotions, and your response is a casual "okay." It might inadvertently convey that you're not fully engaged or, worse, that you're merely waiting for them to finish. This can be particularly problematic if you're distracted, preoccupied with your thoughts, or eager to exit the conversation. In such cases, your "okay" might be interpreted as an affirmation or agreement, even when it's not your intention.

I encourage you to experiment with eliminating "okay" from your repertoire of minimal encouragers. This exercise is not just about avoiding a specific word; it's about cultivating a deeper level of attentiveness in your interactions. By consciously choosing your responses, you become more present in the conversation, ensuring that your feedback aligns with what the speaker is actually saying.

In training sessions, I will illustrate this point by role-playing a situation with Jesse. I might start the conversation with, "Hey, Jesse, I was talking to

Jim, and he mentioned you're going through a tough time with your wife." Jesse, embodying his role, will reply, "Yes, I recently discovered she's been having an online affair for over a year. She's fallen for some other dude in another state and told me this morning that she's leaving me and taking the kids to Arizona."

In the role play, I will intentionally respond with a simple "okay," which escalates the situation. Because of my response, Jesse will become agitated, snapping back at me, "No, man, it's not okay! She's leaving me, taking my kids!" And when I attempt to clarify, saying, "No, no, I didn't mean it's okay," Jesse gets more frustrated and asks me, "Then why did you say it was okay?"

The approach to effectively using minimal encouragement isn't about crafting the perfect response but being genuinely present and engaged. By doing so, you not only enhance your active listening skills but also strengthen the connection and rapport you build with others.

Reflective Mirroring

Having spent over a decade working in mental health, I've heard numerous unique and often bewildering statements from individuals experiencing symptoms of mental illness. These moments underscore the delicate balance required in communication with specific populations. One of many examples of this was a woman from the south side of San Antonio, who frequently called 911 to report various unrealistic occurrences. She insisted that the police helicopter was landing on her roof and the police chief was running a methamphetamine operation in her attic. While she recounted these events with absolute conviction, I knew they were manifestations of her illness. Despite their implausibility, her belief in these delusions was unshakeable, as they were incredibly real to her.

In situations like this, the challenge is to acknowledge and validate the person's experience without reinforcing their delusions. There's a fine line between showing empathy for their perceived reality and inadvertently affirming their unfounded beliefs. This is where the skill of reflective mirroring, or as we sometimes call it, "parroting," comes into play. Much like a parrot that echoes words or phrases verbatim, reflective mirroring involves repeating back what the person has said.

This technique isn't about agreeing with the content of their delusions; rather, it is about acknowledging their feelings and experiences. It's a way of showing you are listening and engaging with their perspective, even when that perspective is skewed by mental illness. By carefully mirroring their words, we open the door to a deeper connection, a critical step in effective mental health communication.

Reflective mirroring is an incredibly effective skill in communication, essential for creating a fluid and meaningful exchange between two people. Typically, an ideal conversation involves a sender and a receiver, with each person taking turns speaking and listening. Remember, the content of our speech accounts for only 7% of our communication. The significance of what we say comes less from our words and more from how they contribute to the flow of conversation.

For instance, imagine a scenario where Person A expresses disappointment: "I'm really frustrated. I saw this great sale on Wagyu beef at HEB and was craving a rib eye steak. But when I got there, the sale was over, and they were all out of steaks." Person B, applying reflective mirroring, would respond with the last few words but with a slight intonation change, almost like a question: "Out of steaks?" This response prompts Person A to continue: "Yes, I guess because of the sale, they sold out of them. So, now I'm gonna go to check a few more HEBs." Again, Person B mirrors Person A's words, this time saying, "A few more HEBs?"

This technique, while simple, is powerful. By repeating the last few words of the speaker, you subtly cue them to continue their story. It's not about interjecting with questions or steering the conversation in a different direction; it's about showing that you're engaged and encouraging the other person to keep sharing. Reflective mirroring is particularly useful if you find yourself lost in a conversation, as it gives you a moment to catch up. It also helps maintain the rhythm and balance of a conversation, ensuring both parties feel heard and valued.

To pose a risky example, let's say you're out to dinner with your partner or spouse. In fact, I encourage you to practice these techniques in a safe space, and what better place than your intimate relationships? Ha. So, I want you to take your partner or your spouse out to dinner tonight or within the next week, and I want you to ask them a simple open-ended question and then pause.

Say this to your partner, "Tell me about your day." As they begin to share, deliberately shift your attention to a different conversation nearby. It's important to understand that we can't simultaneously listen to two separate things. While we can hear and listen, truly listening to two conversations at once is not feasible. The aim is to catch just the last one or two words your partner says. Now, this next part is a bit risky: repeat their words back to them while maintaining eye contact and see if they remain unaware that you weren't fully engaged in their entire story.

This exercise should be done considerately without taking advantage of the situation or being disrespectful. It's merely a method to sharpen your listening skills. Afterward, if you feel confident, reveal to your partner that you were intentionally practicing a new skill from a book you read and explain that you weren't entirely attentive. This can open up an honest and potentially enlightening conversation – or they will launch their hot pasta across the restaurant and storm out of the room. Either way, you will get better at the skill.

The I-Message

The I-message skill is one of my favorites and offers powerful benefits when applied correctly. This technique allows you to express your feelings in response to someone else's situation.

I'm often asked, "Why would others be interested in how I feel, especially if they're strangers?" My extensive experience in community interactions taught me the value of this approach. Even when someone replies, "I don't care," or "I don't give a damn about your feelings," remember not to get fixated on their words. Drawing on Dr. Mehrabian's theory, I appreciate such responses as expressions of their frustration rather than a literal dismissal of my feelings. Contrary to their claims, people do care about how we feel, and this understanding is crucial.

Employing the I-message is especially effective when facing verbal aggression.

Please note: physical violence is never acceptable or condoned. However, when confronted with verbal attacks, an I-message can be an effective response.

The formula for this skill is straightforward: "I feel [insert emotion], when you [describe their behavior or statement], because [your reason]." While you can vary this structure, even placing the "when you" at the beginning, the core elements should remain the same. The I-message is about honestly communicating your emotional response to their actions or words, fostering alignment and connection, and potentially diffusing tension. This approach not only helps convey your perspective but also invites the other person to consider the impact of their words or actions.

If you've seen HBO's Emmy-winning documentary *Ernie and Joe: Crisis Cops* – I am the "Joe" in that, by the way – there's a scene where I talk about a call I had. This woman was married with children, and on this particular night, she waited for her children to go to sleep. Her husband was a licensed firearm owner, and once the family was asleep, she took her husband's gun from the nightstand, went outside, sat in the driveway between two vehicles, put the gun to her head, and called 911.

When I got to the scene, what I saw really surprised me. Patrol officers had heard there was a gun involved, and that one word, "gun," changed everything for them. This is true for most police officers. It's like their training kicks in full force, and rational thinking takes a back seat. The adrenaline starts pumping, logic and reasoning diminish, and they become so fixed on this one thing: "There is a gun, and it can kill me."

The patrol officers were set up down the street. The sergeant on duty called me over and told me about the situation. The scene was pretty intense. There were about six or seven patrol cars, and every one of them had its trunk popped open. Officers were busy loading AR-15s and grabbing shotguns, shields, battering rams – you name it. They were gearing up with just about every piece of equipment they had except for the fire extinguishers. I knew she was sitting in her driveway, so the battering ram really confused me.

The on-scene sergeant asked me what I was thinking. Understanding how scenes like this usually went, I first asked permission to speak freely. He gave me the go-ahead, and I asked him straight up, "Sarge, what's our plan here? Are we really going to march down this street with battering rams and guns, shouting orders at this lady?" He wanted to know what I thought, so I didn't hold back. I said, "Let's slow down and look at what we are doing here. We have one woman threatening to end her life with a gun, showing us how desperate she is. She decided to call the police. She does not want to hurt or kill anyone else, so why are we going to march down the road and confront her?"

I asked if anyone on the scene had tried calling her. Everyone looked at me, puzzled, like my idea was outrageous. Knowing she had a cell phone, as she was on the phone with dispatch, I decided to call her directly. When she picked up, I said, "Brenda, you do not know me, but my name is Joe. I am a cop just down the street from your house, and I assure you I am here to help you."

I asked her to tell me what was going on. She was crying, clearly scared, and poured her heart out to me. I knew I was getting through to her because she stayed on the line. I've had several people hang up right away after I introduced myself. She didn't, further validating that she wanted help.

After hearing her out, I asked her point-blank what she was doing at that moment. She told me she was sitting in her driveway with the gun to her head while her family was asleep inside. I decided to use an I-message and started to tell her how scared I felt, but before I could even finish, she interrupted, asking me why I was scared. She said she didn't want to hurt or kill anyone else, just herself.

I was honest with her. I said, "Brenda, I feel scared when you sit there with a gun in your hand because I am standing next to a group of officers who are loaded to the teeth with weapons, and I am afraid of what will happen if they march down your street."

She asked me what she should do, and I told her to stand up, place the gun on the hood of the truck, and step away from it. I reassured her that I was in plain clothes, that I wouldn't touch her or handcuff her – I just wanted to talk. Just like that, it was over. She complied, and I walked up to her, spoke with her, and, without handcuffing her, put her in my car and took her to a hospital for treatment.

Let's consider the alternative. What if the officers had marched down the street? We have seen this play out too many times. Now we have multiple officers with rifles, handguns, and flashlights yelling, "Drop the fucking gun!" One of three things will happen: one, she drops the gun, and all is well; two, she attempts to drop the gun, but as she is lowering it, one of the officers on the line feels they are being flagged and yells, "Gun!" and the woman is shot 47 times for trying to comply; or three, she shoots herself in the head in front of all of these officers, and now she is dead, and they have yet another traumatic scene to bury in the depths of their souls. Why risk any of this?

This whole situation was resolved because I understood what a person in crisis looks like and was willing to communicate with her. As a male police officer, I wasn't too proud to tell a woman in crisis that I felt scared. My fellow officers need to hear this. In the academy, they drill into us that we should never show fear and that we're never supposed to be afraid. Please allow me to tell you the truth: that is absolutely, unequivocally not true. Almost every aspect of police work is scary. Every traffic stop is scary. Every time you walk into a stranger's home, it's scary. Checking a closed business in the dark after a burglar alarm – scary. Don't trick yourself into thinking you're never scared.

Recognizing that situations are dynamic and there are chances to really connect with people is crucial. By simply admitting, "Hey, I feel afraid right now," or "I'm scared when you move too close to me because I fear you might hurt me," you break away from traditional training. Admitting fear, being vulnerable – is a different approach, but it's one I've used many times with great success. In fact, despite all the people out there telling me how reckless and dangerous I was as a cop – spoiler alert – I didn't die. Not even one time.

Let me share another example. Imagine you're a father, and your 14-year-old daughter comes to you and says, "Hey, Dad, can I talk to you about something?" You reply, "Yeah, sure, sweetheart. What's going on?" She tells you about a new boy at school she's been messaging. She likes him, and he likes her. She describes him as responsible and claims he works in his family business on weekends. Then she says, "Dad, because he is so responsible, he encouraged me to talk to you about getting on birth control."

If you are a father of a daughter, I can sense your discomfort even reading this. There are two ways to handle this. You could get defensive and punish her for being so offensive and asking such an absurd question, or you could use an I-message. You could say, "Lexi, I feel concerned when you come to me about getting on birth control because you are only 14 and I haven't even met this boy."

As a bonus, consider adding a statement of gratitude: "I appreciate you coming to me with this. It shows you trust me, and I do not want to violate that." This approach opens space for conversation, allowing your daughter to feel heard and respected rather than shunned or embarrassed. I-messages are powerful tools in many sensitive situations.

I Can't Imagine

Lastly, there's one phrase I wish all people would eliminate from their vocabulary: "I understand." We should strike this from our vocabulary as much as possible, as it's impossible to fully grasp someone else's experience. Even if you've been in a similar situation, like a car accident with a friend, the death of a parent, or a divorce, each person's experience is unique. Saying "I understand" can unintentionally dismiss the individuality of the other person's feelings and experiences.

The reason an experience or situation is deemed scary differs for each individual. The VA has made significant strides over the decades in understanding what we now call PTSD. In the past, it was termed battle shock or battle fatigue. It is challenging for people to grasp how two people with similar experiences – deploying together, fighting in the same hole, having the same combat exposure, and returning on the same day – can have such different outcomes. One might thrive, starting a family, pursuing education, and building a career, while the other could end up homeless and struggling with addiction. These stark differences illustrate that there's no universal right or wrong in human behavior. It's about understanding individual experiences.

In Chapter 1, we emphasized the absence of good or bad, right or wrong, in human behavior. Seeing situations neutrally helps us support more people effectively. When you tell someone, "I understand what you're going through," you inadvertently minimize their experience. For instance, if a friend is going through a divorce and you've been through one, too, claiming to understand their situation might not be accurate or helpful. Each divorce is unique. The circumstances, the emotional impact, the family dynamics, finances – all of these vary greatly.

There's always what I refer to as an "unaccounted-for variable." So, what should we say instead of "I understand"? Try replacing it with "I can't imagine." This simple change can be incredibly powerful. It shows empathy without assuming you fully grasp their unique experience. It acknowledges the uniqueness of their situation and opens a space for them to share more about their feelings and struggles. When we do this well, we validate their feelings without imposing our own experiences or judgments. If you can relate, great. I used my life experience and struggles to connect with the people I was helping every day. But it does not mean I could ever understand what they were feeling or going through. I can relate, but I can't imagine.

For instance, suppose you're consoling a friend grieving the loss of their parents. I experienced the pain of losing my father several years ago, sadly, at the young age of 53. When consoling someone in a similar situation, I might say, "While I, too, have lost a parent, and it was incredibly difficult for me, I can't imagine what you're going through." This statement acknowledges that while you share a similar experience, you recognize their grief is unique and personal. It conveys empathy without assuming you know exactly how they feel. It's about relating to them on a human level while respecting the individuality of their experience.

This approach is incredibly beneficial because it allows the person to feel their emotions fully without being pressured to conform to a specific way of feeling. It avoids creating a power dynamic or making someone feel like their grief is somehow less significant because you "understand" it. Instead, it leaves space for their emotions and validates their experience as unique.

For all leaders, regardless of profession, it's crucial to remember that we are all in the business of dealing with people. The faster and better we grasp these skills, the more effective we become in our roles. Reflect on each interaction you have. Use those bookends: start with curiosity, asking yourself, "What else could be true?" and conclude by evaluating your contribution to the outcome. If the interaction went well, it's likely due to your effective use of active listening skills and the MOREPIE approach. If it didn't go as planned, it might be an indicator to refine these skills.

Remember, mastering these techniques takes time – give yourself about 18 months to fully comprehend, practice, and integrate these skills into your interactions. This patient, consistent approach will enhance your ability to connect and communicate effectively with those around you.

Understanding the power and principles of effective communication and active listening will undoubtedly help you level up your life, just as they have helped me. Effective communication and empathy are an undefeated dynamic duo. Sure, going 11 years without using force in a large police department is great, but so is seeing how skills I used to talk people out of barricaded situations or off a bridge when they were contemplating ending their life transfer to starting, running, and growing my business, SolutionPoint+.

Communication is connection, and the more we connect, the more we can relate to one another. The more we can relate to each other, the less scary it is to love one another. The less scary it is to love one another, the better off everything will be.

CHAPTER 4

My Great Epiphany

"The first step in healing is to not be angry with others."
~ Seneca

When giving keynote talks, I often share how I measure success in my life, something I realized after listening to Dr. Joe Dispenza on Tom Bilyeu's podcast, *Impact Theory*. Dr. Dispenza mentioned an interesting fact: by the time we are 35 years old, 95% of our daily life has become a series of automated, habitual routines. That was a real eye-opener for me. It made me see the importance of breaking free from the daily grind to ensure my tomorrows weren't just carbon copies of my yesterdays.

CURRENT STATE OF MOST PEOPLE

I invite you to take an assessment of your life right now. Is tomorrow going to look exactly like yesterday? Will next week copy last week? Will next month look like last month? For most people, the answer is an easy yes. This does not maximize our human experience.

This insight came to me at a pivotal moment in my policing career, in its final 18 months. Despite the gratification I found in helping brother and sister officers and making a significant impact nationwide with SolutionPoint+, I still felt off-balance.

In 2019, I had the honor of speaking at an NYPD law enforcement suicide-prevention symposium, addressing police executives from around the world. Yet, back in my department, I felt stifled and unheard. Why? In my view, there's an unspoken rule, especially in larger police departments like the SAPD: you are only allowed to be as smart as your rank. This realization was a crucial part of my journey, shaping my understanding of true success and my desire to break away from being controlled by poor leadership. As author Marcus Buckingham said in his book, *First, Break All the Rules: What the World's Greatest Managers Do Differently*, "People leave managers, not companies," this was absolute truth for me.

This combination of factors – police departments led by emotionally detached men lacking the necessary skills, insight, and leadership; my wellness proposals being routinely rejected; and the tragedy of three suicides within our department over 18 months – left me profoundly frustrated. My best friend, Jesse, who has been by my side for 24 years and is president of SolutionPoint+, often observed how uncharacteristically negative and miserable I had become. Thank goodness for therapy, which has played such a pivotal role throughout my life – shout out to Dr. D!

My therapist gave me the courage to end my 15-year policing career. For reference, you are unable to draw a pension until you work for at least 20 years. Leaving five years shy of pension eligibility was not a common practice, especially in San Antonio, where the police department has one of the strongest pensions in the country. I see many first responders who feel imprisoned by their pension, stuck and unhappy yet unwilling to make a change. Without my therapist, I'm certain I'd still be at SAPD, probably miserable, counting down the days and years to a minimal 20-year pension. In the last three years with my business, I've achieved what might have taken another 15 to 25 years had I stayed and played small.

I wrote this chapter to challenge you to break free from your routine and do something that ensures tomorrow isn't just a repeat of yesterday. Consider this book your key to unlocking the shackles of the monotonous 95% and embracing the opportunity to explore and expand the dynamic 5%.

MY PREFERENCE FOR US ALL

It's crucial to remember that life is a balance of 50–50 – for every sunrise, there's a sunset; every inhale is met with an exhale. This is the polarity of the universe, a dance of give and take. Our focus often lies too heavily on achievement and success, on constantly climbing without realizing that this pursuit is invariably accompanied by its opposites: failure and struggle. Life is not meant to be a smooth journey.

We should be encouraged when we realize how it all works, knowing that every setback has an equal climb. I often wonder what would have happened if the police chief in San Antonio had actually supported the HBO documentary *Ernie and Joe: Crisis Cops*, which he approved to be made, by the way. I wonder what would have happened had he not ordered his command staff not to support the film or any requests coming into the department for me to speak.

I was essentially benched for doing nothing wrong, yet I have no doubt it was the very thing that led me to take the leap and bet on myself. That chief makes it into my gratitude journal more than he will ever know. I am now able to control my own destiny, write my own story, and go where I am called and valued. There have been so many moments over the last few years that have encouraged and inspired me, moments that I would not have experienced had I not left my job.

I want to emphasize how problematic the idea of leaving a law enforcement job early can be for some people. SolutionPoint+ collaborates directly with the Federal Bureau of Prisons. On the morning of the first day of a three-day training, Jesse and I were doing our normal introductions to the class, establishing our backgrounds and credibility. I mentioned that I had recently (at the time) left my career as a police officer in San Antonio and discussed what we were doing now as a company. At the end of the third and final day of training, the Bureau requires all attendees to go to a computer lab to take a test and fill out a survey.

We are then provided with those test scores and the class assessments for review. I was pretty shocked when I read one critique from a gentleman (I know it was a man because his coworkers and vanpool sold him out to me): "As soon as I heard Joe and Jesse quit their jobs after 15 years of policing, that tells me they are dirty, crooked, and corrupt cops." Wow. Not much surprises me anymore, but that one really did.

I, of course, preferring to handle things maturely, went to the front of the group just before graduation and addressed the class as a whole. I said, "I would love to have a conversation after class with whoever wrote this feedback to understand your perspective. I'm not angry; I'm just confused and curious and would love to discuss this with whoever wrote it." True to my experience of rarely being surprised, the person who wrote the feedback did not come forward to speak with me, choosing instead to leave with the group without addressing it personally. It's unfortunate. But it highlights the level of disruption it can cause when someone learns a first responder has chosen to leave for their own sanity or personal reasons. We must do better.

One of SolutionPoint+'s most impactful offerings is a two-day, 16-hour course called "X-Factor Mental Wellness and Resiliency," developed after I left SAPD. You'll start to see a recurring theme here. We were conducting this training in a small Iowa town. On the first day, Jesse led a session on post-traumatic stress and PTSD, discussing symptoms and experiences. During this session, an officer bravely shared his story in front of his peers and other first responders. He detailed his struggle over the past eight months, including thoughts of ending his life and the reasons that had led him to such a dark place. Jesse acknowledged and appreciated his openness, creating a truly profound moment in the class.

On the second day, I was leading a segment on wellness and resiliency, similar to what you'll find in the last chapter of this book. Part of the session involved a gratitude practice, where each participant received a gratitude journal. This was a new concept for many officers in the room, as they hadn't used such journals before. After guiding them through their first entry, I invited anyone willing to share something they were grateful for. This practice was designed to highlight a key point.

One officer volunteered, saying, "I know it might sound cliché, but I'm actually grateful for this class." I assured him it wasn't cliché and expressed my appreciation for his participation. He continued, "No, you don't understand. The officer who opened up yesterday about his struggles is my best friend, my partner. I'd take a bullet for him, yet I had no idea about the depth of his pain. Thanks to your training, he felt safe enough to share his story. Over lunch today, I confided in him something I've never told anyone else. This training and your approach created the space for that to happen, and for that, I am truly grateful."

As I listened to the officer's story, I was deeply moved. A profound sense of pride stirred within me – not pride in what we were doing, but in his courage to open up in front of his peers. That level of bravery is exactly what we need to foster in the first responder community.

Marketing our business and setting prices for our services has been a challenge, especially when considering the impactful feedback we've received. Hearing from countless first responders in the last three years, with comments like, "I had lost all hope and thought about ending my life, but your training this week gave me hope," "Your training helped me release some demons that were haunting me," and "There is no doubt your work is saving lives; I am proof of this," reinforces the vital importance of our work.

These testimonials deeply resonate with me and the entire team. They're the reason we push so hard in our mission. Yet, it's sobering to realize that many first responders are still unaware of our existence. I don't say this to paint a rosy picture or simplify the complexities we face. The journey is daunting, filled with as many setbacks and failures as there are successes. But when we understand that our own beliefs and limitations are the only true barriers, we discover an incredible sense of freedom.

I've never been one to boast, "Look at me, follow my lead." In fact, I often advise the opposite. I've made plenty of mistakes, making life more challenging than necessary, and I'm still learning how to overcome these hurdles. I aim to light the way for those who feel broken, torn down, or defeated. I hope my story, with its trials and victories, inspires others to persevere.

Positive psychology research underscores the influence of mindset on our physical and mental health. Challenges are not setbacks but opportunities for triumph. As Ryan Holiday beautifully states in his book *The Obstacle Is the Way*, the barriers we face can be the very path to our progress and success.

Remember, it's not about the accolades or the heights we reach but the depth of our experiences and the courage to face our fears and embrace vulnerability. Whether you're a first responder, a business leader, a parent, or anyone navigating the complexities of life, know that your struggles are your strengths in disguise. They are the crucibles that forge your character.

I hope that these words not only resonate with you but ignite a spark to embrace your journey, with all its ups and downs, and see your challenges not just as hurdles but as stepping stones to a stronger, more resilient you. We should never look back and wish things away or that they were somehow different. Remember, whatever happened, no matter how difficult, was meant to happen, and no amount of fighting will ever change that. We are left with two options: finding the lesson or embracing the pain.

As anyone who knows me will attest, my story is an open book, and I've never claimed to have all the answers. The discovery of Stoic philosophy and my ongoing therapy have transformed my life. I'm far from perfect – I still face struggles, as I have for most of my life.

By the age of 33, I had been through three divorces and fathered four children with three different women, yet as a member of a mental health unit, I was advising others on how to best live their lives. I was the epitome of a hypocrite, and because of my years serving as the CHO (Chief Hypocritical Officer), it is so easy for me to spot this trait in others.

I've made numerous mistakes, and I fully accept responsibility for them. They were my choices and no one else's fault. Even now, as I write this book, I continue my journey of treatment and healing. I anticipate this being a lifelong process, and I'm completely at peace with that.

CHAPTER 5

Follow the Thread

"Amor Fati" [Love your fate].
~ Friedrich Nietzsche

Law enforcement in the United States has a complex and somewhat troubled history, and recent years have arguably been among its most trying periods. Over the last 18 years, I have immersed myself in the culture of law enforcement, working closely with various agencies across the country. My experiences have been crucial for the development of my skills, particularly during my tenure with the San Antonio Police Department. I have deep gratitude for the opportunity and lessons learned there.

Most law enforcement agencies, including SAPD, are making commendable efforts to adapt to the dynamic needs of their communities, yet perfection remains a distant goal. It is not lost on me that the challenges are immense in an agency with over two thousand sworn officers. Personally, I have been involved in training all of them at all ranks, including crisis-intervention team training, de-escalation, and mental health updates during in-service training. I've gained a rich understanding of not just policing but human behavior as a whole.

As an aside, the underrepresentation of women in law enforcement is a critical issue. Currently, women constitute about 13% of the workforce in this sector. Various initiatives, such as the 30 by 30 Campaign, aim to increase this percentage to 30% by the year 2030. However, achieving this target is daunting, considering the challenges inherent in the recruitment, hiring, and training processes.

But let's go deeper into the essence of law enforcement personnel. Who are the individuals who choose to don a gun belt, carry a badge, and exercise significant power and authority over others? Why would someone willingly embrace a profession that routinely involves navigating danger and distress? Have you ever paused to reflect on why you chose this path – or whichever path you are on?

Regardless of your current role, function, or profession, it's crucial to understand the motivations behind your career choice. Not everyone ends up in the profession they envisioned as teenagers. For some of you, maybe your current role aligns with your youthful aspirations, which could be beneficial or perhaps limiting. I encourage you to think about this: are you where you truly want to be, or is there a different path awaiting your exploration?

The Adverse Childhood Experiences Study (ACEs), conducted decades ago, has its critiques, but for a moment, let's take its findings at face value. While primarily a public health tool for predicting potential adult health or behavioral issues based on childhood experiences, I believe it can also shed light on the identities we forge.

These identities, much like the hand-me-down clothing we discussed in an earlier chapter, can be shaped by the burdens of childhood traumas. Often, survival skills developed in tumultuous childhoods are mistakenly adapted as strategies to thrive in chaotic adult environments. As my therapist tells me, structures are formed. First responder roles, with their inherent turmoil and uncertainty, can sometimes mirror these childhood experiences. The safety we seek is often found in chaos that does not serve us.

It's important to clarify that not all, or even most, police officers in America had challenging childhoods. In many areas, like Iowa and parts of Illinois outside Chicago (where SP+ has done a lot of work), the majority of officers come from stable backgrounds. This is not a knock on them by any means. I truly wish we were all zeros on this ACE assessment. However, my experiences have shown a different picture in larger cities.

For instance, while conducting the ACE training in San Antonio, I observed that around 70% of officers had an ACE score of four or higher, which is considered high by the study's standards. My own ACE score is a nine. This realization brought clarity to me: it was never a matter of not knowing right from wrong. One of the principles I teach is that no amount of childhood trauma excuses ignorance of the difference between right and wrong. But a higher ACE score often correlates with an increased apathy towards consequences, a truth I've experienced firsthand. Our habits and behaviors create consequences that often validate our experiences of ourselves.

Another challenge I've noticed, both in myself and others, is the desire to wear a mask, concealing our true emotions and who we truly are. In high school, I was nicknamed "Smiley," yet I wrestled with my first suicidal thought at 15. Growing up in a volatile, unstable, and unsafe environment can delay the development of empathy. This observation isn't limited to first responders; I believe it has implications across various professions. It raises critical questions about how our early experiences shape our professional lives and interactions. It shows up in leadership, or the lack thereof.

Obviously, I am not the first to see and understand this issue. I am not trying to convince anyone that I have discovered some groundbreaking theory that would even make Jesse Trevino (my scholarly BFF) jump on his bed. What I am trying to do is bring awareness to a specific population (first responders) and gently remind them that maybe it isn't everyone else's fault for why they are so unhappy, frustrated, calloused, angry, and/or depressed. Maybe they truly did not know any better, and this can be their invitation to pay attention to the emotions being stirred inside them, even if it is disgust at reading this.

Professions, at their core, are made up of people. Wherever there are people, similar issues and behavioral patterns inevitably surface. This is particularly true for men in leadership roles. If you're a leader with an ACE score of 4 or higher and have never sought therapy or professional help, with all the love I have in my heart, you are wrong. Become more self-aware and follow that thread.

Our beliefs, behaviors, and feelings are often tied to our childhood. No amount of professional success, wealth, or promotions can erase or compensate for your past. The events that shaped you were not your fault, but addressing them now is your responsibility. Too often, I've witnessed leaders wielding their power as a shield against introspection, using their authority to mistreat others rather than lead with empathy. This is especially prevalent in policing, where promotions are often based solely on memorizing a book to take an annual test, and promotions are directly correlated to test scores without regard to merit, character, or interpersonal skills. An incredibly flawed system, to be sure.

The absurdity of this system is highlighted by an experience I had assisting an officer grappling with suicidal thoughts, struggling to navigate an inadequate support system. When I advocated for this officer to a deputy chief – a top-ranking officer with over 30 years of service – the deputy chief's response was dismissive. He said, "Joe, if I ever find out that there is a man or a woman in my department who is too mentally weak to do the job, I don't want them in my uniform." Such a statement not only troubled me but also reinforced the challenges I faced in advocating for officers' mental health – often having to work around such archaic mindsets.

I told him, "Well, Chief, you just made my job that much harder because now I need to find a way to help these officers without you ever finding out about it."

Our company's mission to eradicate suicide among first responders, starting with police officers, is hampered by these outdated attitudes. The belief that "the best thing is just to outlive the dinosaurs" is not enough. We need a culture, mindset, and leadership shift that encourages vulnerability, supports those who are struggling, and refrains from punishing or discarding them. I challenge leaders to confront their past and embrace the potential for transformation. This change is crucial for individual growth and the betterment of the entire profession and those in your charge.

Remember, what you experienced as a child wasn't your fault. However, as an adult, it's entirely up to you to confront and work through these issues. You owe it to yourself and those who look up to you. It's time to take off the mask, embrace your own story, and confront your pain and struggles. Use the strength you gain from your healing journey to connect with others. I can assure you, it's a path worth walking.

I believe a big part of why people connect with me is my openness about my flaws and my refusal to offer excuses. I recognize that my past actions, while misguided, were forms of self-sabotage stemming from my insecurities and the healing I still needed. This is something I am still dealing with today. How can we expect to be surrounded by love and respect if we don't first show it to ourselves?

So many of us are assholes to ourselves. I, for sure, can be. I carry a great deal of guilt, shame, disappointment, and pain because of the choices I've made in my life. It is not my mother's fault. It is not my father's fault. It is all my fault. And because it was easier to validate the hate I had for myself than to accept that I was the problem, I continued to make poor choices that made life more difficult. Thankfully, after multiple versions of a breaking point, I began to heal my past. It was after I started my healing journey that I was then able to honor and admire my scars.

Too often, we surround ourselves with people who echo our past pains, repeating patterns that do us no good. Now is the time to stop merely covering up these old wounds with temporary fixes. It's time to address them head-on, pull out the splinters of our past, and begin the true process of healing and growth.

Remember, real empathy comes not from claiming to understand someone else's experience but from recognizing that you cannot truly know what they are feeling yet still choose to support them. I mentioned in the book's introduction the significance of this work to me, and I shared that my ACE score is a 9. For those familiar with the ACE assessment, this means I experienced all but one of the listed traumas.

My parents got married at a very young age, and my father served in the Navy. I have an older sister who is three years older than me. During one of my father's deployments, my mother engaged in an affair with another sailor. This sailor came to the house frequently and sexually abused me. This went on for quite some time. At one point, I confided in my mother about what was happening. Her response was dismissive: "We don't talk like that." As a confused seven-year-old, I couldn't process this.

One weekend, in our base housing in Norfolk, while my sister was in the bathtub and my mom, a smoker at the time, was asleep on the couch, I snuck a book of matches from my mother's purse. I crawled under my bed and tried to set it on fire, but the matches wouldn't ignite. Finally, one match stayed lit and caught the fabric underneath the mattress on fire.

In a total panic, I rolled out from under the bed, pounded on the bathroom door, and yelled for my mom. We all rushed out of the house as my mother called for a fire response. Not long after, the base fire department arrived and swiftly extinguished the fire. Thankfully, there wasn't catastrophic damage – just my bed caught fire, leaving some charred floor and wall.

As I stood outside, uncertain of what would happen next, a fireman approached me. He bent down, looked straight into my eyes, and sternly warned, "Young man, if you ever start another fire again, you'll spend the rest of your life in prison. Do you understand me?" His harsh tone made me burst into tears as I realized the gravity of my actions.

I have no anger or ill will towards this firefighter – or any firefighter. But as a seven-year-old, I wish he had shown empathy instead of threatening me for my behavior. I wish he had offered hope or help. How incredible it would have been if he had just graduated from SolutionPoint+ training the week before – or even read this book and decided to implement the CCRTC model.

This incident highlights the kind of leadership we need and the kind SolutionPoint+ teaches. When we approach situations introspectively, we can replace judgment with curiosity. Instead of threatening those in our care, like our children or community members, we can offer them help and hope. That's all I was seeking that day and what I strive to provide now. It is my literal "why." It is why this work matters so much to me. I want to help the next child who cries for help, even if we don't understand or agree with how they are doing it.

CHAPTER 6

Change Your T-Line, Change Your Life

"The happiness of your life depends upon the quality
of your thoughts." ~ Marcus Aurelius

You might be familiar with Viktor Frankl's profound quote from 1946: "Between stimulus and response, there is a space, and in that space is our power to choose our response." This concept, foundational to Cognitive Behavioral Therapy (CBT) developed in the late '60s and early '70s, revolutionized our understanding of the mind. Similarly, Charles Swindoll's oft-quoted saying, "Life is 10% what happens to you and 90% how you react to it," has been shared over 65 million times globally, emphasizing our control over our reactions.

My argument has always been that Stoic philosophy is the foundation of life coaching, but some may disagree. These historical insights are not to be understated; they highlight the immense power we hold in shaping our experiences. In this chapter, let's tap into that critical pause, the fleeting yet pivotal gap between what happens externally and our response to it.

The focus here is to empower you to recognize and master this space, to realize you can control it to serve your best interests. In these brief, often-overlooked moments, our mindset is both forged and fostered. I'd like to provide strategies to help you harness this space, guide your decisions, and chart the course of your future.

Back in 2019, when Jesse and I were still part of the police department and our business was two years in, a mentor advised us to seek a federal contract as a growth milestone. Jesse diligently searched online for opportunities and came across an RFP from the Department of the Navy in Hawaii requiring "mindset shift training." At first, I was unsure of what this entailed, but it resonated with our ongoing work in mental health and the wellness and resiliency work we had started doing.

We started the rigorous process of creating a competitive proposal, only to realize as the deadline approached that our offering and current capability were perhaps only about 70% aligned with the task. Undeterred, we submitted our best and final offer, eager to see if our understanding of mindset transformation aligned with the Navy's expectations.

As this was our first attempt at securing a federal contract, we found ourselves navigating unfamiliar territory when asked for our BAFO (best and final offer). Consulting with mentors, we learned it likely meant we were one of the final contenders and were now competing on price. We were advised to reduce our bid by 5%, so we adjusted our proposal to just under $900k. Ultimately, we didn't secure the contract. The winning bid, shockingly, was double ours at $1.8 million. This other company, already serving giants like Apple, the NFL, and Facebook, had the established infrastructure and experience we lacked. They were fully prepared to fulfill the contract's requirements while we were still learning the ropes.

This was a pivotal moment in our business. I had gotten a small taste of being close to a big job, yet the reality was that we failed. We did not win the bid, but it enriched our journey. It motivated us to go harder and develop a deeper understanding of what the essence of "mindset" even meant. Had we won the contract, the learning curve would have been steep and immediate.

In the wake of this setback, I faced a choice: to give up and whine about not winning or learn from the experience and rise stronger. Inspired by Yogi

Berra's wisdom, "When you come to a fork in the road, take it," I embraced the challenge. I wanted to move beyond superficial understandings, past the motivational posters and company slogans. I sought a profound grasp of mindset, not just as a collection of beliefs but as the lens through which we view the world and engage with its myriad challenges and opportunities. Does this sound familiar, echoing what I said in the first chapter? I hope so. It all ties together. This quest led me to appreciate the concept of life coaching, which may be overused today but not always fully understood.

The STEAR Model

During this time, I was walking the greatest dog to ever bless this planet, PJ (my 85-lb. English Cream Goldendoodle), with my wife, Jessica. She was telling me all about this coaching program she was in and how they use a CTFAR (Circumstance, Thought, Feeling, Actions, Result) model (credit to Brooke Castillo) as the "self-coaching model."

Now, I know there are a ton of mixed reviews out there about the entire coaching industry, but I am giving credit where it is due. As I listened to my wife talk about this model, I thought, *How can I take that and make it into something more "cop" or "military friendly"?* That is when I thought of the STEAR mindset framework – a powerful tool for reclaiming agency over one's life and directing outcomes.

Enter the STEAR Model: *Situation, Thoughts, Emotions, Actions,* and *Results* (yes, I know that is not how you spell steer). While an argument can be made about the difference between emotions and feelings, my goal here is to introduce these concepts to a general audience without causing confusion. For the purposes of the STEAR framework, I use emotions and feelings interchangeably. For more on what a feeling/emotion is, read below.

S – Situation: The situation refers to external, factual events. It is neutral and includes the actions of other people. For example, stating "The temperature is 108 degrees," is a fact, whereas saying "It's hot outside" is not a fact. The situation itself has no inherent meaning until we form a thought about it. Additionally, the situation does not directly cause our feelings or emotions; our thoughts about the situation do. While it might be tempting to believe that your boss saying "You could have done better" in front of all your colleagues is the source of your anger or frustration, the real source of your feelings is the thoughts you have about the neutral facts (i.e., your boss said words).

T – Thought: This is what you think about the situation. You likely have several thoughts about any given situation, but only include one thought per STEAR model instance. A thought is a single sentence or phrase in your mind that assigns all the meaning to a situation. This one sentence is also the source of the subsequent feeling or emotion.

Using the example above:

- Situation: Boss said, "You could have done better," in front of six other people.
- Thought: *He has no respect for me.*
- Emotion: Anger.

The distinction between the Situation and Thought is huge because we do not have control over every situation, circumstance, event, other people's behavior, but we do have control over our thoughts and the story we tell ourselves about the situation, circumstance, event, and other people's behavior. Thoughts are not facts, and thoughts are optional. We may not be able to control the thoughts our brain offers up, but we do have the power to choose which ones we hold on to, play on repeat, and look for evidence to support and reinforce.

E- Emotion: An emotion is a vibration in your body that comes from a thought in your brain. An emotion is one word. If someone asks how you feel and you respond with a sentence, you are sharing a thought.

For support in identifying the one-word emotion you are experiencing, refer to the feelings wheel shown:

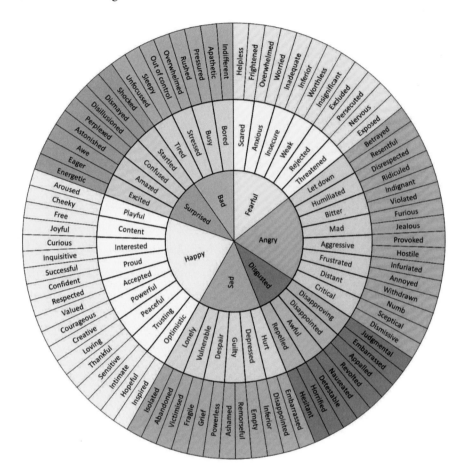

Sample of a feelings wheel.

Emotions are incredibly important because they drive your behavior and actions. Everything we do or don't do, all our actions, inactions, and reactions, stem from an emotion or from an attempt to avoid an emotion.

While many of us avoid it, learning to identify, feel, and process an emotion is the foundation of taking control of our lives.

A – Actions: Actions are what you do or don't do from the emotion caused by your thoughts about the situation. While only one thought and one emotion should be included in each model, it's useful to list *all* of the actions, inactions, and reactions coming from the thought and emotion combo so you can clearly see the result you create.

R – Results: The result is the effect of your actions. The result will always be evidence of the thought. Note: only you should show up in the *Results* line of your STEAR model. The goal is to bring awareness to what *you* are creating in your life.

To recap, Situations are neutral until you have a *Thought* about them. *Thoughts* give the *Situation* all the meaning they have and create the *Emotion* you feel. The *Emotion* drives the *Actions* you take. The *Actions* (or inactions) create the *Results* you have in your life. This framework helps create awareness of what is creating your emotional experience, how you're showing up in your life/relationships/career/etc, and the results you are creating. In short, it helps you see what you are creating with your thoughts.

Let's look at an example of default thinking vs designed mindset using the STEAR framework.

DEFAULT THINKING	DESIGNED MINDSET
S. Boss assigns a task you've never done.	**S.** Boss assigns a task you've never done.
T. I don't know how.	**T.** I'm figuring it out.
E. Confused.	**E.** Curious.
A. Mental rumination: focus on what I don't know, don't research, don't ask questions, don't trial and	**A.** Identify what I **do** know, identify what I don't know, hypothesize possible

error, don't fail, and learn from mistakes. **R.** I don't figure it out.	solutions/options, try one, evaluate (what worked, what didn't work, what can be done differently), apply learning to next attempt, ask for help when needed, allow "failing"/learning and keep trying. **R.** I learn something new. I figure it out.

DEFAULT THINKING	DESIGNED MINDSET
S. Your spouse tells you they quit their job. **T.** They should have talked to me first. **E.** Anger. **A.** Yell, blame, threaten, look for evidence of other times they did things wrong, don't ask questions from curiosity, don't offer support. **R.** I don't communicate well with my spouse.	**S.** Your spouse tells you they quit their job. **T.** I hope they're ok. **E.** Concerned. **A.** Ask questions (i.e., How are they feeling? What happened? What do you need at this moment?), listen, share concerns, talk through options and possibilities, discuss next steps **R.** I stay connected to my spouse.

This framework is a fundamental approach to reshaping how we interact with our world. It encompasses responsibility and can guide our internal narratives, which, in turn, influence our actions and reactions to both hurdles and possibilities. The exploration of mindset is not just theoretical; it's about practical application, about "STEARing" our lives with intention and purpose.

Harnessing the power of introspection to transform automatic or habitual reactions into deliberate responses is key to mastering our challenges. Viewing every challenge as a learning experience and an opportunity to develop resilience is a mindset shift that I encourage you to embrace and practice. By adopting this approach and integrating it into your daily life, you'll soon discover the profound impact of maximizing your human experience.

The STEAR model, which I learned from listening to my wife, is something I have implemented myself. I'd even go as far as to say I am a testament to its transformative power. To be very clear, of the two of us, she is the only certified life coach. I try very hard to use these skills and concepts on a daily basis in my marriage, parenting style, and business. It was so enlightening for me personally that SolutionPoint+ started including a class during our two-day X-Factor Mental Wellness and Resiliency training.

Consider the common frustration of being stuck in traffic, a scenario we've all faced. For me, the congested roads of San Antonio, particularly I-35, have been a frequent challenge. In such situations, your perception and reaction are critical. You could yield to annoyance and stress, leading to aggressive driving and arriving at your destination in a flustered state. Or worse, you might encounter road rage from an unhinged citizen who clearly has not read this book yet.

But what if you reframed the situation, shifting your mindset to transform your experience, leading to a more composed and productive state upon arrival? Instead of viewing traffic as a frustrating obstacle, see it as an unexpected opportunity to engage in a productive or enjoyable activity, like listening to an audiobook, catching up on a podcast, or simply using the time for some mental preparation or reflection. This mindset shift could not only alleviate stress but also transform a potentially negative experience into one that is calming and beneficial.

This type of response fosters a sense of control and peace, even in situations that are inherently out of our control. It exemplifies the power of perspective – how a situation that initially appears to be a setback can be reimagined as a valuable moment of pause in our often hectic lives. This approach, while seemingly simple, can have far-reaching, positive effects on your day-to-day well-being and overall approach to life's inevitable delays and detours.

The STEAR model is equally valuable during heated arguments. Instead of viewing an argument purely as a conflict, recognize it as an opportunity for resolution. This shift can change your emotional response and actions, leading to more positive outcomes. In relationships, it boils down to a simple choice: do you want to be right, or do you want to maintain love and connection? You often can't have both.

This model emphasizes the importance of adjusting our internal responses rather than trying to control external circumstances. It's about "STEARing" our life's course with intention, turning challenges into opportunities for growth, and every interaction into a chance for better understanding and connection. As Seneca wisely stated, "If a man knows not to which port he sails, no wind is favorable."

Now let's apply STEAR to a law enforcement situation, like responding to a domestic disturbance call. These scenarios can be complex and fraught with danger. Without the STEAR model, an officer might instinctively respond to hostility with defensiveness or aggression, escalating emotions and potentially worsening the situation. However, by applying the STEAR model, the officer can approach the situation with a mindset geared towards de-escalation and understanding, leading to safer, more constructive outcomes. This approach is not about compromising safety; rather, it's about enhancing situational awareness and response effectiveness. Nothing I, or any SP+ Facilitator, will ever teach is to make you less safe, I assure you.

Typically, such situations escalate into a use of force, potentially resulting in injuries, complaints, or, in the worst cases, lawsuits or fatalities. Conversely, if the officer adopts the STEAR model, they might recognize the volatility of the situation but realize it's not entirely within their control at that moment. While officers are trained to immediately manage environmental chaos, this approach can sometimes be too literal, leading to a brief suspension of common sense. This is precisely why the STEAR model is highly relevant and timely for police officers across the country. It offers a smarter, more thoughtful alternative to the outdated method of asserting authority and expecting automatic compliance.

Returning to our example, the officer applying STEAR shifts their thought process toward curiosity and empathy. By considering the potential stressors affecting the couple, they achieve a more balanced emotional state. This influences them to use a softer tone, active listening, and genuine empathy. The result? A de-escalated situation where the officer can effectively mediate the couple, potentially fostering a peaceful resolution.

Consider one more common law enforcement scenario: the traffic stop. An officer pulls over a driver who immediately shows anger and non-compliance. Without STEAR, the officer might respond with mirrored aggression, escalating the situation, which could lead to an unnecessary confrontation or even violence. However, by applying STEAR, the officer maintains control over their thoughts and emotions, approaches the situation calmly, and employs the CCRTC model of de-escalation. This approach can defuse tension, leading to a safer outcome for everyone involved.

Gone are the days when the old ATM method – ask, tell, make – is acceptable. In today's world, and rightly so, this approach is no longer viable. Many updated alternatives are being taught to law enforcement agencies throughout the United States. I propose that STEAR be taught, too. In my view, it's the most effective and beneficial method for officers in high-tension situations.

One of the latest methods I heard about before I left San Antonio was the LEED model: Listen and Explain with Equity and Dignity. Officers are trained to take the time to listen to people, explain what is going to happen and how the process works, explain why that decision was made so the equity of the decision is transparent, and leave the participants with their dignity intact. This model seems lovely, but to me, it still seems quite one-sided, and most officers lack the introspection to see they have escalated a situation.

I wear a compass pendant around my neck every day. It is temporary until I find the right tattoo artist to get the image I want on my arm. It is a reminder for me about what I need to do to find my true north. I will discuss that more in the last chapter, but I want the STEAR model to serve as a compass for you, helping you navigate the complex and unpredictable landscape of whatever you are facing. It should empower you to approach every situation with a new skill that pushes you to embrace the introspective mindset. It truly can enhance your safety. I want to remind you that I did not learn these skills until after I left law enforcement, yet I was able to go my entire mental health policing career without using force, meaning one is not contingent on the other.

My success in policing came from using the CCRTC model. I learned STEAR after, and I use it daily in my life, my business, and as a father and husband. When we learn to master our thinking, we can also learn to master our emotions, actions, and results. For first responders, the skill helps you better serve your communities with the dignity and respect those communities deserve.

For any non-first responders, please don't miss the opportunity to leverage this mindset in your leadership style. Maybe you're wondering how this model can help you as a leader in your business. I've got you. Let's say you've missed a critical deadline due to unforeseen technical issues. Without STEAR, you might react impulsively and blame the project team, leading to a tense atmosphere. This escalates emotions of fear and resentment among the team, resulting in defensive actions and a lack of collaboration. The project suffers further delays, negatively impacting company performance and team morale. As they say in South Texas, "No Bueno."

With STEAR, you can recognize the setback as a situation beyond your immediate control, allowing you to focus on constructive thoughts and view it as an opportunity for problem-solving and team growth. This leads to determination and collaboration, prompting actions such as convening a solution-focused meeting with the team. The outcome is a collaborative effort to resolve issues, leaving the team feeling supported and motivated and potentially leading to innovative solutions and stronger team cohesion.

Let's take another example: navigating organizational change. The situation is an organization undergoing a significant restructuring, causing uncertainty and anxiety among employees. Without STEAR, an executive might ignore the emotional climate, focusing solely on the logistical aspects of the change. This oversight could lead to increased anxiety and disengagement among employees, resulting in decreased productivity and possibly higher turnover.

However, with STEAR, the executive can acknowledge the situation's complexity and focus on empathetic and transparent communication. This approach fosters a sense of understanding and security among employees, leading to actions such as open forums for discussion and feedback. The result is a smoother transition with engaged employees who feel valued and heard, enhancing the success of the organizational change.

These are just a couple of high-level examples on the corporate side to show the versatility of this model. You really can plug any situation into this model to help manage professional challenges and foster a more positive culture. I have no doubt that if your organization understands and uses this model, it will enhance collaboration and cohesion and positively impact the culture of your workforce.

I was watching an episode of *Impact Theory* (yes, I reference Tom Bilyeu's show a lot because I am all for giving credit where it is due) several years ago, and he was wearing a shirt that said, "Everything is my fault." I loved it immediately and adopted it as one of my many mantras in life. It does not mean you deserve to be victimized in any way. What it means is you are absolutely required to identify and handle your shit. Nobody else is responsible for how you feel.

Whatever happened to you as a child was not your fault, but here's the good news - if you're reading this book, clearly, you survived it. Now it is on you to overcome your old structures, decide who you want to be, and then make it happen.

I may not get to tell my brain what to think immediately or habitually, but I absolutely get to tell it what to focus on. We all have our default settings, but it doesn't just stop there. We get to reprogram the entire system whenever we decide and commit to it.

Don't be afraid of your feelings or emotions. They really are there to serve you. Your emotions are the language of your subconscious, and they are there to teach you something. Do not suppress them. Pursue and get to know them. You may just become really good friends with yourself. What a concept that would be.

CHAPTER 7

Worthy of Tomorrow

"Suicide doesn't end the chances of life getting worse, it eliminates the possibility of it ever getting any better." ~ Unknown

This chapter addresses a topic of profound sensitivity and importance, and I feel it's essential to begin with a clear disclaimer. We will be discussing the grave matter of suicide, a subject that can deeply affect many. If you or anyone you know is grappling with suicidal thoughts, I cannot stress enough the importance of seeking professional help immediately. While this chapter aims to provide informative and empathetic insights, it is not a replacement for the guidance and intervention of qualified mental health professionals.

I share this content with the utmost respect and passion for those hurting the most, recognizing that introspection, self-discovery, and self-awareness are vital tools in our journey. As someone who leads a company dedicated to removing the stigma surrounding mental health, I want to acknowledge that everyone's experience is unique and significant.

I have battled with suicidal ideations since I was 15. This is an ongoing journey for me, one that I navigate with the support of my therapist. But before I go any further, I want to highlight some crucial resources. This list isn't exhaustive, but it includes some key avenues for immediate support:

- National Suicide Prevention Lifeline: 1-800-273-TALK (1-800-273-8255)
- Suicide and Crisis Lifeline: Dial 988 (Available 24/7 in the United States)
- Crisis Text Line in the U.S.: Text "HELP" or "HOME" to 741741
- For international resources: Visit IASP.info
- In case of immediate danger: Call emergency services or head to the nearest emergency room

Depression and Anxiety

Before we explore the aspects of suicide assessment, it's important to grasp the intricacies of depression and anxiety. These are two of the most prevalent mental health diagnoses globally, and their prevalence isn't just due to genetic predispositions. When thinking about anxiety and depression, I encourage you to consider various contributing factors that go beyond genetics.

If you turn on your television to watch the news, which I would never encourage doing, you will see massive amounts of suffering and chaos. It's easy to see how your mood is directly tied to your media consumption. What you watch, read, and listen to all contribute to how you feel. Sometimes, the best thing we can do to make ourselves feel better is to shut off or change our media consumption habits.

Let's examine what anxiety and depression are in the most basic terms. Put simply, anxiety is the fear of a made-up future. It's our brain crafting stories about what might occur, be it in the next five minutes or next year. This kind of thinking generates internal stress about events or situations that are yet to unfold –the essence of an anxious mindset. Remember, my intention here is not to offer a self-diagnosis; professional guidance is always recommended for that. My goal is to enhance our collective knowledge of these common mental health conditions.

While anxiety is the fear of a made-up future, depression can be viewed as an inability to let go of the past. To illustrate this, in our company training sessions, I often use the metaphor of a pendulum swinging back and forth.

When you wake up in the morning, where does your mind wander? For many, as soon as their eyes open, they're already dreading something about the day ahead, a classic symptom of anxiety. Others might wake up still entangled in feelings of anger, hurt, or frustration about something that happened yesterday. This is where depression comes into play – it's when we're caught in the grip of past events despite the fact that they are behind us and unchangeable.

This discussion is not about diminishing or ignoring our feelings. Quite the opposite – I encourage you to engage deeply with your emotions. It's about elevating your emotional intelligence, understanding where your thoughts tend to veer, and learning to manage them more effectively. By recognizing these patterns, you can begin to address your responses to both past experiences and future uncertainties, something we refer to as "minimizing the sway." Even the most healthy of humans, mentally or otherwise, will notice when their brain is future-tripping or past-dwelling, but I want us to learn to recognize it faster, realize what is happening, and minimize the unnecessary pain because of it.

To truly grasp what your emotions are communicating, let's consider the moments just before sleep when our minds are most genuine and unguarded. Every night, as we settle into bed – regardless of our sleep environment, whether it's filled with the hum of a TV, the presence of someone else, or solitude – there's a brief period just before you drift off. In these moments, our conscious guard drops, and our minds wander freely, often reflecting on the future or revisiting the past. This pre-sleep state is a window into our authentic selves, undistracted and raw. So, tonight, as you're on the cusp of sleep, I want you to think about me… Okay, I agree; I can make things weird at times (HA!). But I do want you to take a moment to observe where your mind wanders.

Instead of letting your thoughts spiral into worries about tomorrow or regrets about yesterday, shift your focus to gratitude. Imagine how transformative it would be if our last waking thoughts were filled with appreciation. Reflect on the comfort of your bed, the security of your home, and the warmth of your blankets. Appreciating the little things we take for granted -= your ability to not just buy this book (if you did) but read it, too. Be thankful for your health and the peace of your current state.

Embracing gratitude in these moments can help diminish our tendencies to worry about the future or cling to the past. It's about finding balance, and as Dr. Susan David wisely noted, suffering is an inherent part of a life well lived. By focusing on gratitude, we can not only minimize our worries but also enhance our appreciation for the present, creating a more grounded and satisfying life experience.

In the realm of life's challenges, it's an undeniable truth that suffering and loss are experiences shared by all, regardless of how virtuous we might be. It's crucial to acknowledge that these difficulties shouldn't shatter, harm, or overwhelm us. When discussing symptoms of depression, especially among first responders, it's instructive to refer to the *DSM-5*, the *Diagnostic and Statistical Manual of Mental Disorders*. My conversations with first responders have led me to categorize these symptoms into three distinct levels, as outlined in the *DSM-5*. Examine the accompanying graphic, focusing particularly on the middle and right pillars, and you will see that these symptoms are remarkably common among first responders, even those who appear to be managing their lives well.

SYMPTOMS OF DEPRESSION

- Despondency
- Inadequacy
- Dejection
- Suicidal Ideation
- Hopelessness

- Irritable Mood
- Difficulty Sleeping
- Change in Eating Habits
- Mood Swings
- Anger

- Social Isolation
- Frequent Sadness
- Loss of Energy
- Grief
- Loss

Many first responders struggle with many of these
** Never diagnose yourself - always seek professional help **

The prevalence of these symptoms is not meant to encourage self-diagnosis but to highlight their widespread nature. I also want to dismantle any notion that being diagnosed with depression or taking antidepressant medication disqualifies someone from being a highly effective first responder. Throughout my career, I've encountered many first responders who were on medication for depression. I, too, was on antidepressants at two different times while serving as a police officer. What's important is having the insight to recognize when something is amiss, the courage to address it, and the acceptance of medication as a form of assistance – if a medical professional has suggested its use. I also admit there are forms of medication-resistant depression. I would never say there is any one right way to address all people and their complex needs.

When I was a cop, I preferred to work alongside first responders who understood their mental health needs and took steps to manage them rather than those who, despite obvious signs of struggle, chose to ignore their issues, potentially making them a liability in high-pressure situations. As a community and a society, we need to strive to eliminate the stigma surrounding mental health, especially in professions where mental resilience is constantly put to the test.

This shift in perspective and approach to mental health is crucial for the well-being and effectiveness of our first responders. We have to stop believing we can have it both ways. Somehow, and much to my disbelief, there are still people – both inside and outside of first responder professions – who truly believe that if a person struggles with mental health at all, they are unfit for duty.

It's essential to grasp a fundamental aspect of mental health treatment: the majority of prescriptions for psychotropic medications aren't typically written by psychiatrists but by general practitioners or family doctors. This detail underscores the widespread impact and complexity of mental health issues.

When it comes to antidepressants, there's a crucial point to understand: these medications generally take four to six weeks to become effective. Unfortunately, due to a lack of awareness about this, many individuals prematurely cease their medication after only a few days, often influenced by a fleeting moment of feeling better. This sporadic usage fails to yield the full benefits that these medications are designed to provide.

The most effective approach to treating depression combines some form of psychotherapy or talk therapy with medication. However, it's important to recognize that medication isn't a universal solution. There are therapeutic alternatives, such as Alpha-Stim and Eye Movement Desensitization and Reprocessing (EMDR), offering different paths to recovery for those who might not respond well to traditional medication.

Now, let's turn our attention to anxiety, the other most commonly diagnosed mental disorder worldwide. Before we jump into our SP+ method of suicide assessment, it's important to acknowledge how highly unlikely it is for someone to take their own life without being afflicted by anxiety or depression. Learning some of the precursors to such a tragic decision is key to preventing suicide. Anxiety manifests in various forms, from generalized anxiety disorder and panic disorders to specific phobias, separation anxiety, and obsessive-compulsive disorder. People suffering from these conditions often experience a pervasive sense of dread, an impending feeling of doom, or even sensations akin to suffocation. These intense emotional states can profoundly affect their ability to function and cope with daily challenges.

For those who have experienced or know someone who has suffered from panic attacks, the intensity of these episodes can be alarming. The sensation of suffocation or feeling as though you're having a heart attack is a profound testament to the potent effects of anxiety on our bodies and overall system.

When considering the global impact of anxiety, many people focus on absenteeism – the failure to show up for work on time or perform effectively while there. However, research indicates a more significant concern: presenteeism. This term refers to individuals who are physically at their workplace but mentally disengaged. This issue becomes particularly critical in the context of first responders.

Imagine a police officer undergoing a personal crisis, such as a divorce, child custody dispute, or civil litigation. They might be struggling with a lack of sleep, poor nutrition, excessive work hours, and a contentious personal life. Yet, due to staffing shortages, their request for time off is denied. Consequently, you have an officer patrolling the streets who is grappling with their personal turmoil and lacking adequate support from their department. In such a scenario, even a routine traffic stop can escalate quickly.

This isn't to excuse any behavior but rather to highlight the reality many face. In my travels across North America, conducting training sessions, I often remind attendees that although they are physically present, their minds might be elsewhere, dealing with personal crises ranging from relationship issues and financial woes to health scares. This lack of full presence can have a ripple effect throughout their agency and the community they serve.

Regarding the treatment of anxiety, a common approach involves the use of benzodiazepines. However, this class of medications poses significant challenges due to their highly addictive nature and potential for misuse or abuse. Prolonged use of benzodiazepines, followed by abrupt cessation, can have severe, even fatal, consequences – a risk shared only with alcohol. This underscores the importance of cautious and informed management when treating anxiety with these substances, highlighting the need for comprehensive care and support for those grappling with anxiety disorders.

We must approach the treatment of anxiety with careful consideration, especially in terms of the medications prescribed and their effects. Looking at the data on suicide, particularly in the context of the COVID-19 pandemic in 2020, offers some intriguing insights. In March 2020, when COVID-19 was officially declared a pandemic in the U.S., we faced unprecedented challenges nationwide. Interestingly, despite a significant increase in mental health diagnoses during this period, there was a 5% reduction in suicides compared to 2019.

I hypothesize that Americans display remarkable strength and resilience in the aftermath of crises. Historical events such as the bombing of Pearl Harbor in 1941, the 9/11 attacks in 2001, and the onset of COVID-19 in 2020 show a pattern where Americans become more communal, friendly, neighborly, and supportive of each other. This tendency to come together in times of crisis reflects our inherent communal nature. However, this sense of unity is often short-lived, as we soon revert to our routines and habits, leading to disconnection.

Suicide

This fluctuation in communal support and connection may explain why, despite an increase in mental health issues, there was a decrease in suicide rates in 2020. However, as I predicted, this trend was like a pendulum destined to swing back. Indeed, in 2021, there was a 4% increase in suicide rates from

2020, and in 2022, the rate increased by another 3.8%, resulting in 49,449 suicides in the U.S. This brings the average to about 130 suicides per day, a staggering figure that underscores the pervasive nature of this issue.

Furthermore, and more personal to me, it's crucial to recognize that the most significant risk factor for police officers in America is not the external dangers of the job but the internal battles with unprocessed trauma and mental health issues. Tragically, police officers are more likely to die by suicide, often using their service weapons, than to be killed in the line of duty. This alarming fact has been consistent for years and highlights the urgent need to address suicide and mental health within the law enforcement community. We must acknowledge and confront the reality that suicide remains a critical issue that requires our immediate attention and action.

It's precisely because of the gravity and complexity of suicide that I am deeply committed to this topic. For me, it's crucial to address the importance of language in discussing this sensitive subject. As part of our mission to dismantle the stigma surrounding mental health, our company advocates for a shift in the terminology used when referring to suicide. Traditionally, phrases like "committed suicide" or "completed suicide" have been common, but there has been a significant change in perspective since 2019. However, many people are still using these outdated terms. We now advocate for the term "died by suicide" to convey the event more neutrally and respectfully.

Language matters immensely in this context. The term "commit" is often associated with crimes, while "complete" typically refers to achievements like running a marathon. By using these terms in relation to suicide, we unintentionally ascribe either a negative or a positive connotation to it. Our goal is to remove such biases and view suicide neutrally. It's not an act to be celebrated or condemned; it is a tragic event that "just is." This perspective is vital for fostering understanding and empathy.

Furthermore, it's essential to recognize that the person experiencing the crisis defines its nature and gravity. It's not our place to judge whether someone's crisis is valid or significant. What we've learned about suicide is that most people who die by it don't actually want to end their lives. They're seeking an escape from unbearable pain or a seemingly hopeless situation. They often experience tunnel vision, focusing solely on finding a way out of their distress. This point is critical when offering support and assistance. There is hope in the fact that many seeking to end their lives are actually longing for a change in their circumstances, not death itself. Our approach should always be rooted in this fact and encourage us as we offer help and support to those in need.

The profound impact of suicide attempts and the insights from those who have survived them cannot be overstated. This was poignantly illustrated by Kevin Hines, one of the few survivors of a jump from the Golden Gate Bridge. I was giving a keynote in 2019 at a conference where he was the other speaker and got to hear his testimony. His revelation immediately after he jumped, while freefalling at roughly 75 miles per hour, was that no one would know he didn't actually want to die. That resonated deeply with me, and I had chills when I heard him say that.

This sentiment was echoed in my experience as an officer in the mental health unit, where I encountered heart-wrenching situations, such as the tragic case of a 15-year-old who hanged himself in his closet. The despair and grief of his mother were overwhelming, particularly the cries she let out as she realized she did not have the strength to lift her child off the clothes bar. I had to pull her away so I could lift him enough to unravel the dog leash he had used to end his life.

The aftermath of such incidents often leaves families grappling with a mix of emotions. In this particular case, the boy's mother later expressed to me her struggle to find peace, believing her son had wanted to die. While this belief might offer some solace to those left behind, it's crucial for those of us in intervention roles to approach these situations with the belief that the motivation for suicide is often less about a genuine wish for death and more about an intense need for change or escape from current circumstances. This perspective can be pivotal in our approach to intervention, helping us break through the tunnel vision that can consume those contemplating suicide.

When considering why people take their own lives, several risk factors come to light. Stressful life events, a family history of suicide, financial strain, trauma, and exposure to suicidal behavior are all significant contributors. These factors can create a complex web of despair and hopelessness, leading people to view suicide as their only escape. It's essential for us as caregivers, first responders, or simply compassionate human beings to understand these dynamics and approach each situation with empathy, seeking to provide the support and change that might be desperately needed.

The impact of witnessing suicide as a first responder is profound and far-reaching, affecting dispatchers, paramedics, firefighters, police officers, and corrections officers. The frequency with which first responders encounter the aftermath of suicide can lead to a troubling level of desensitization. Throughout my police career, I attended countless incidents where people had tragically ended their lives, some leaving notes, others communicating their final thoughts through texts. Each scene was a stark reminder of the pain and finality of suicide.

I recall one particularly distressing experience involving a fellow officer in San Antonio. This officer was under immense stress and anxiety, struggling with family issues. I managed to get him connected with my therapist at the VA, even becoming a part of his care continuum with his consent.

A profound lesson came one day when my therapist advised me to start mourning the loss of this officer, predicting his eventual suicide. Initially, I was angry and in disbelief. How could a therapist say something so definitive?

When the officer did tragically take his own life, it shattered me. Seeing him at peace, knowing he had found his way out of his suffering, left me with an eerie feeling. It resonated deeply with my struggles with suicidal ideation, making it all the more impactful. On this day, I realized the significance of boundaries. I learned a hard lesson: no matter how much love, encouragement, support, care, or kindness you give someone, people will always do people things.

Over my career, I've been called to scenes of suicide by various means: gunshot wounds to the head, chest, or stomach; hangings; jumps from great heights; overdoses on drugs or medications; self-inflicted cuts; and even carbon monoxide poisoning. Each method carries its own haunting image, a vivid memory that remains indelibly etched in my mind. The accumulation of these experiences has left me with persistent intrusive thoughts, a vivid testament to the harrowing nature of the job and the critical need for mental health support.

I left SAPD in 2020 and still battle the intrusive thoughts and memories as if I just got off a shift this morning. Experiences like these drive my advocacy for therapy and professional help, not just for myself but for all first responders who are repeatedly exposed to such traumatic events. Seeking professional help is vital to process these experiences and manage the emotional toll they take. It's a journey of healing, of acknowledging the burden and finding a way to bear it while still moving forward.

When faced with the possibility that someone close to you – be it a colleague, friend, or family member – is experiencing emotional distress or exhibiting signs of depression, active listening skills are crucial. It's vital to engage in a manner that extends beyond merely hearing, focusing on not only what is explicitly stated but also on the unspoken cues, particularly body language, which accounts for 55% of communication.

Often, signs of distress can be overt, with individuals expressing thoughts of ending their lives or feeling like a burden, saying things like, "I'm going to end it all," or "My family would be better off without me." Other times, the indicators are more subtle, perhaps simple but loaded statements like "I'm just tired." Such a statement is not a cue to discuss sleep patterns but an invitation to probe deeper with thoughtful, open-ended questions.

Understanding that fleeting thoughts of suicide are, according to research, relatively common is essential. Brief considerations like, "I can't handle this anymore," or "I wish I wouldn't wake up tomorrow," are not immediate causes for alarm, but they shouldn't be ignored, either. They are opportunities for engagement, gentle inquiry, and offering support. What's crucial is maintaining a calm and composed approach. Panic or overreaction can exacerbate the situation, potentially closing off lines of communication.

Effective intervention, whether as a professional, friend, or family member, hinges on normalizing conversations around mental health and suicide. Being comfortable in discussing these topics can significantly ease the other person's anxiety about sharing their feelings. It creates a safe space for honesty and openness, which is critical for providing the support and help they may need. Remember, the simple act of showing genuine concern and willingness to listen can often make a profound difference in someone's life.

The SP+ Assessment Triangle

In conducting a suicide risk assessment, certain key strategies can significantly enhance the effectiveness of your approach. Being direct and confident in your questioning is vital. One crucial point to remember is to not be satisfied with an initial no when you ask someone if they are considering suicide. Often, people in distress may deny having suicidal thoughts due to fear of judgment, reluctance to share, or not fully recognizing their state of mind. This is where the SP+ Triangle, a framework we've developed and successfully used thousands of times throughout my 15 years in law enforcement, becomes invaluable.

This triangle is designed to simplify the assessment process amidst the plethora of conflicting methods out there. The key lies in persistence and a methodical approach. After acknowledging the initial response of the person considering suicide, continue the conversation but revisit the question later. The second time around, employ the "PNA technique": *Paraphrase, Normalize,* and *Ask.*

Imagine that a friend is confiding in you about their divorce, financial struggles, potential loss of child custody, sleep deprivation, and excessive drinking. Now, suppose that when you ask, "Do you want to kill yourself?" they hesitate but eventually respond with a no. Acknowledge their answer but maintain the conversation.

When revisiting the question, use the PNA method. Paraphrasing means repeating back what they've shared with you, which helps validate their feelings and shows that you're actively listening. Normalization means reassuring them that it's okay to feel overwhelmed in such challenging situations, helping to reduce any stigma or shame they might feel. It also gives them an opportunity to not feel alone if you remind them, "Anyone going through as much as you are right now might think about killing themselves." Finally, ask them again, with care, concern, proper tone, and empathy, if they are considering suicide. If they are, they are far more inclined to open up and be honest with you about it.

Using this approach, you create a safe space for honest dialogue. Your tone of voice is crucial here – it needs to be empathetic, non-judgmental, and supportive. The goal is to make them feel heard, safe, and not alone in their struggles. Through this method, you're not only assessing their risk but also offering them a lifeline of support, compassion, and connection.

For example, I could approach a friend and say, "Hey, listen, I know I asked you earlier if you're thinking about killing yourself, and you said no, but here's what I'm hearing. Your spouse is leaving you, she's taking the kids, and since she's been the breadwinner, now you're facing the loss of your house in the divorce. I just want to tell you that it would not be uncommon for someone going through as much as you are right now to have thoughts about suicide. So, I need to ask you again, and please be honest with me: are you thinking about killing yourself?" Paraphrasing their situation, normalizing their feelings, and then re-asking the critical question opens up a space for an honest response. People aren't likely to lie about their feelings, especially if they sense genuine concern and empathy. I've relied on this method numerous times, always beginning with a direct question once I'm aware or suspect what they might be experiencing.

I'll use a good I-message to start with, like, "I can't imagine what you're going through right now." Then I might say, "Listen, what you just said there concerns me. I've got to know; do you want to kill yourself?" If they say, "No," beautiful. We keep talking, and then I go back to the PNA. "Hey, I know you told me you didn't want to kill yourself, but what I'm hearing you say is…" Paraphrase their words into one, two, or three bullet points and then normalize, which gives them an out: "It would not be uncommon for anyone else going through as much as you are now to be having thoughts of suicide. I just need to know." Only then do you ask them about suicide again. The PNA should open them up to an honest response.

So, you might be wondering, *What is the SP+ Triangle?* It's simply a three-sided, three-question framework. They're individual questions, intentionally. Do not combine them. Treat the SolutionPoint+ (SP+) Triangle as a precise sequence that must be followed in the order of 1, 2, 3 – not in any other combination, like 2, 3, 1, or 3, 1, 2, or 1, 3, 2. It's crucial to adhere to this order: first, ask question one and then pause; proceed to question two and then pause; and finally, ask question three. Allow time for a response after each question.

The first question is straightforward: "Do you want to kill yourself?" It demands a clear yes or no answer. This question is designed to be closed-ended and is only posed when there's a presumption or anticipation that the answer might be yes. A common barrier to asking this critical question is the fear of receiving a yes as an answer. My objective is to alleviate this fear. Understanding that this fear is normal is key, but it's essential to ask nonetheless to provide timely and potentially life-saving intervention.

When addressing the sensitive topic of suicide, it's imperative to approach it with both directness and sensitivity. The first step, as part of the SP+ Triangle, is to ask, "Do you want to kill yourself?" This direct question is essential, and we should be prepared for a yes response but not fear it. This anticipation guides us to ask the question with the intent to provide help. The second step is to ask, "Do you have a plan?" This question is also typically closed-ended, as responses can range from a simple yes or no to divulging specific details about their plan. For instance, if someone affirms they want to kill themselves and adds, "I plan to shoot myself," the subsequent question naturally becomes, "Do you have access to a gun?"

Similarly, if an individual expresses a desire to overdose on medications, the follow-up question should be, "Do you have access to these medications?" It's crucial to understand that not every expression of a desire to die by suicide equates to the possession of the means to do so. Many times, individuals may not have the resources to enact their thoughts, but this does not diminish the seriousness of their intentions. It simply means they are contemplating suicide but lack the means to actualize it.

If someone says they don't have a specific plan, it's not necessary to proceed with the third question about means. The key is to address each step based on the responses given. It's also important to remember that the most common methods of suicide include shooting, hanging, overdosing, or jumping off something. However, not all self-harming behaviors, such as cutting, are necessarily suicide attempts. Often, they are expressions of emotional pain and trauma, a way to feel amidst their suffering. This systematic approach helps to assess the risk and urgency of the situation effectively.

After completing the SP+ Triangle, it's crucial to maintain engagement. This is not the time to switch topics to hobbies, the weather, or other unrelated subjects. Once you reach this level of intimacy and they are opening up to you, be grateful but also stay engaged. Continuing to collect information becomes paramount, as you might only have this one opportunity to make a difference.

For instance, if you've completed the triangle by asking, "Do you want to kill yourself?" and they've answered affirmatively, told you that they plan to use a firearm, and confirmed having a gun in their possession, it's essential to dig deeper. Keep the conversation focused and build on the rapport that has been established. Ask pertinent questions to better determine their state of mind and circumstances. This approach is not just about assessing the immediate risk but also showing genuine concern and providing the support they need at that moment.

Expressing gratitude is crucial when engaging in conversations about suicide. When someone shares their suicidal thoughts, acknowledging their trust in you is vital. For instance, when I ask someone if they are contemplating suicide and they respond affirmatively, I make it a point to thank them for their honesty. For the greatest impact, use I-messages to convey this appreciation. Recognize the significance of their willingness to share their most daunting fears with you, and never underestimate the power of gratitude.

After completing the assessment triangle, I often say, "Thank you so much for sharing that with me. I can't imagine what you're experiencing right now." This leads to further questions, like, "Have you ever attempted suicide before?" This inquiry aims to uncover any pattern of behavior.

Another important question is, "Has anyone in your family ever died by suicide?" Here, we're looking to tie in family history. Also, asking, "How long have you been thinking about killing yourself?" helps gauge the intensity and duration of their thoughts.

Finally, a critical question to ask is, "What has been keeping you alive until now?" If someone tells you they have been thinking about wanting to die for a week or three days, ask them why they haven't done it yet. This seeks to identify their protective factors – the elements that have sustained them and could be pivotal in their ongoing safety and well-being. This must be done with the proper tone and an empathetic energy.

Now, some people might think that's a harsh question. I'm not challenging them to go through with the suicide – I'm seeing if they know what their protective factor is. And guess what? Ninety-nine percent of the time, they do. Once they tell me what it is, I use it to break through their tunnel vision. I say, "Hey, you've been thinking about killing yourself for five days. Why haven't you done it?" Their response is usually, "I can't imagine doing that to my kids." And there it is. We now have our protective factor. I know I'm going to be able to intervene and help them.

It's important to remember that even successful interventions in a crisis don't guarantee a permanent resolution. Often, individuals are most vulnerable to suicide right after an intervention or being discharged from treatment. This crucial period necessitates our vigilance and continued support to ensure they remain connected to their community and don't feel isolated. Recognizing the nuance and complexity of suicide is fundamental to fostering safer and more empathetic communities. Every action we take, no matter how seemingly insignificant, can profoundly affect those battling despair.

While this chapter may be activating for some, it paves the way for the next chapter, which emphasizes the significance of cultivating our mental and emotional well-being. This isn't just about preventing crises; it's about building a life enriched with purpose, joy, and resilience.

Prioritizing wellness and self-care is a commitment we owe to ourselves and is indispensable for healing, personal growth, and the thriving of our shared human experience. It's an invitation to embrace a form of beneficial self-focus and prioritize your well-being, not just for your own sake but for the collective good. This is more than self-care; it's a call to become the best version of yourself for the benefit of all.

CHAPTER 8

Reclaim Yourself

"Everything is my fault."
~ Tom Bilyeu

W hen did we transition from human beings to relentless human doings? This chapter cuts through the fluff to present a straightforward guide on wellness and resiliency, underscoring the necessity of putting yourself first. Imagine that! I am asking you, as I demand for myself, to become more selfish. Pause for *GASP*.

In today's world, where overachievement is often celebrated, and life's pace only seems to quicken, many of us are misled into thinking that self-care is an indulgence we can't afford. Let's be clear: that is complete bullshit. Prioritizing your well-being, bolstering your resilience, and focusing on your overall wellness are not just beneficial – they are essential. In an "others-centered" world, I ask one question of you: to what end?

It's long past the time for us to change our perspective, shifting from a constant state of doing to a more intentional state of being. We should reevaluate and redefine our standards of success, extending beyond professional achievements to include the quality of our personal lives. This chapter is a call to action, urging you to embrace self-care not as an act of luxury but as a fundamental necessity for a balanced, fulfilling life.

Let's explore the art of reclaiming our individuality in a world that incessantly prescribes our identity and actions. Embracing selfishness is not solely for personal benefit; ultimately, it enriches those around us. There is a vast difference between being selfish to serve yourself and being selfish to better serve others. For many years, I've harbored a desire to transform the messaging on every police car in America to a simple yet powerful slogan: "Prioritizing me to better serve you." While some may raise eyebrows at this notion, its truth is undeniable. Think about it.

First responders nationwide are in a constant cycle of service, often facing mandatory overtime and denied leave, only to find themselves in hot water for a misstep or a misworded statement caught on camera. I wish we would slow down and conduct what I like to call a "situational autopsy." We must examine and understand the consequences of constant service without self-care.

So, how can we serve without first ensuring our own well-being? It's crucial to understand that by taking care of ourselves, we are better equipped to care for others effectively and compassionately.

My Time as a Mental Health Trainer

One of the standout achievements in my career was in 2020 when I was honored to lead the mental health refresher training for the San Antonio Police Department, a mandatory course required every three years. In November and December of 2019, we meticulously prepared the learning objectives to deliver this crucial training. Every Tuesday, I had the privilege of teaching this eight-hour mental health class. However, I noticed the material had not been updated since the last time we taught it.

Quick side note. As I mentioned earlier, in 2019, I had the distinct honor of being invited by the Police Executive Research Forum (PERF) to speak at an officer suicide prevention symposium in New York City at NYPD

Headquarters. This event gathered 350 police leaders from across the globe, and my insights and voice contributed significantly to the discourse. However, upon returning to San Antonio, my efforts to advocate for improvements within my department were met with consistent denial. This frustration was compounded by the sobering reality that we had witnessed three suicides within our department over 18 months.

This experience underscored a challenging truth I've observed in many police departments: one's influence is often constrained by one's rank. Clearly, this was something I had a problem with as I refused to be a good boy and kiss the ring of the "leader." Don't get me wrong, I spent 20 years, my entire adult life, in service – honorably. I was never disciplined or punished for being disrespectful or insubordinate, but that does not mean I stood by without a voice and lay down, either. I care way too much about people to blindly follow ignorance.

I knew we were scheduled to teach the mental health updates at our in-service sessions, but I also knew we had a unique opportunity to reach the entire agency. I proposed an idea: what if I could dedicate the last 90 minutes of every Tuesday to a segment on wellness and resiliency tailored specifically to our department? Despite submitting the request, I never received a formal response, so I proceeded with the plan anyway, curious to see the outcome.

In the second week of the in-service training, a deputy chief attended my class. Post-session, he commended me on the impact of the class and encouraged me to continue. I took the opportunity to inquire if he could facilitate official approval of my request to teach it. He simply reassured me, "You're doing a good job," so I persisted.

From January until COVID-19 led to the academy's closure in March, and then from its reopening at the end of June until my departure on September 24, 2020, I taught this 90-minute block on wellness and self-care. I developed this module based on my own lived and learned experiences, and I titled it "Six Pillars of Self-Care."

The response was profound. After each session, officers would wait for the crowd to dissipate before approaching me with their personal crises: suicidal thoughts, struggles with addiction to opiates or pornography, habitual excessive drinking, and even being under the influence while on duty. The raw honesty and vulnerability these officers displayed, their willingness to reach out for help, was heartbreaking. It was a stark reminder of the urgent need for mental health support within the first responder community. We needed help.

In conducting just this one training block, I learned an invaluable lesson that profoundly influenced my career trajectory. It became glaringly obvious that we were facing a significant problem within the department. Moreover, I recognized that my potential to make meaningful change and offer substantial assistance would be exponentially greater if I stepped away from my current role. This would allow me to extend my reach to other agencies and organizations where my skills and dedication would be more appreciated and effectively used. I was terrified, but I knew I needed to take the muzzle off.

Tragically, the urgency of this issue was further highlighted by a somber statistic: six officers from the San Antonio Police Department died by suicide within a mere seven-month span in 2021, a stark indication that the situation was worsening. I am not taking credit and associating the increase in suicide with my departure from the agency the year prior, but I can say the amount of suffering in our department and the massive lack of trust in leadership is obvious.

It's critical to understand – and I urge you to absorb this point – IT IS NOT ABOUT RESOURCES. I have repeated this tirelessly over the years, yet it often seems to fall on deaf ears. The emphasis I place on being selfish stems from this very realization. It's about curing the pervasive disease to please others at the expense of one's well-being. It's about reclaiming control over your life.

I want to clarify that this issue is a common one and not unique to any department. The challenge lies in the cultural and systemic barriers that prevent resources from being leveraged to support the mental health of our officers.

As an illustration, let's consider the San Antonio Police Department. They are well-equipped in terms of support systems, with three full-time psychologists dedicated solely to officers and their families. Additionally, a peer support team of over 50 members is available for officers. The department also boasts a full-time mental health unit catering to the community and officers and a chief's wellness unit designed exclusively for officer well-being. Despite these ample resources, six officers died by suicide within seven months. This clearly underscores that the issue at hand transcends the mere availability of resources.

So, if the root of the problem isn't a lack of resources, what is it? The answer lies in the culture – and by that, I mean "big C" culture. The crux of the matter is trust, or rather, the lack thereof. Officers may hesitate to use these resources due to a lack of trust in departmental policies and administration and the absence of a precedent or established practice that encourages open and honest usage of mental health resources. This is a widespread challenge, not unique to any single department but prevalent across many in the country. Each situation is distinct, and no two departments face identical issues. It's a complex, multifaceted problem, and resource availability is just one piece of a much larger puzzle.

Most agencies improvise on the fly when it comes to handling officers or employees in crisis. Many lack concrete policies for such situations. Simply providing an employee assistance program (EAP), a toll-free helpline, or a flyer on a bulletin board is not enough. What's really needed are internal champions – individuals who have navigated through their own dark moments, experienced despair, sought help, and emerged thriving on the other side.

This was the role I embraced at the San Antonio Police Department. I never shied away from sharing my struggles with PTSD, suicidal thoughts, relationship woes, multiple divorces, medication, and the various challenges and failures I encountered. My openness about these personal battles, I believe, drew many towards me. They saw in me a figure of courage and vulnerability, someone who did not pretend to have all the answers but strove for betterment. I didn't tell people what they needed to do but shared what I was doing. I was in the trenches with them – not above, not better, but truly with them.

I have a general rule when it comes to "authenticity": if you have to tell people you are authentic, maybe you actually aren't. But this is a book, so stick with me here. I believe my authenticity resonated deeply with many.

The Six Pillars of Self-Care

Now let's briefly explore the six pillars of self-care, a course that has become highly sought after across the country, particularly during COVID-19, when virtual engagements became more prevalent. These sessions highlighted the urgent need for improved wellness and self-care in organizations and industries.

It's intriguing to consider what "wellness" and "resiliency" mean to different people. Your definition of these concepts might vary significantly from that of the next person reading this book. While there may be overlaps, the individual nuances in understanding these terms underscore the diversity of our experiences and perceptions in the realm of mental and emotional well-being.

Wellness

The definition of wellness is often described as a state of good health, particularly when it's a goal actively pursued. However, I want to simplify this for better understanding. Wellness boils down to two words: "active pursuit." It should invoke the idea of active engagement.

Yet, here lies a common pitfall in human thinking: we often mistake wellness for the acquisition of material or external goals. We tend to think, *If only I achieve this [specific goal], then I will feel [a certain way].* This could be anything – obtaining a degree, finding a partner, buying a house, getting the dream job, or earning a certain amount of money. We believe these achievements will bring us the desired emotional state.

However, this satisfaction is usually fleeting, leaving us wondering why the feeling of fulfillment didn't last. This is because true wellness isn't about acquiring things or reaching external milestones. It's crucial to understand that we are, at this very moment, as complete and fulfilled as we can be. Wellness is about recognizing and appreciating our current state rather than perpetually chasing something external in the hope that it will bring us lasting happiness or fulfillment. It's about finding contentment and purpose in the journey itself, not just the destination.

I realize it might be tough to hear, but we've all hit a plateau in our lives. Right now, you are at the peak of your abilities based on your current state of being. For some, this realization might be perfectly acceptable, but for others, like myself, it's not quite enough. I've realized in the last few years that to improve and grow, I need to transform myself. This means engaging in new experiences, reading more, engaging in deeper conversations, embracing failure, and experimenting with different approaches. If I allow my days to mirror each other, with no variation or growth, I know exactly where I'll be in the future: right where I am now. And that's not where I want to be.

If you're content with where you are, that's great, and I genuinely celebrate that with you. However, if you're like me and striving for more, it's crucial to acknowledge that our journey is about transformation. It's not solely about the end goal, the achievements, or the material gains. It's about the journey of personal evolution – who we need to become to reach our desired destination. Embracing this concept means understanding and appreciating our capacity for change and growth. It's about enjoying the fluid, dynamic nature of our personal development and recognizing the beauty in our ability to constantly evolve and adapt.

Resiliency

Let's get into the concept of resiliency, generally understood as the ability to bounce back swiftly from challenges. However, the definition often includes the word "toughness," which I find somewhat misleading. When we hear "tough," our minds conjure images of physical strength – muscular builds, athletic endurance, or powerful bodybuilders. But when it comes to first responders, I'd argue we have done a terrible job of defining the term. We think it's about enduring the emotionally taxing and distressing events of the day. We think being "tough" means shutting our mouths after a hard day, suppressing all of our feelings, and moving on like nothing happened.

Many first responders are all too familiar with heart-wrenching calls, such as responding to a tragic car crash involving a young child. After handling the immediate aftermath, completing the necessary reports, and finishing a demanding shift, they're expected to return home as if nothing happened. They're supposed to sit at the dinner table with their family and remain emotionally present. Then, they must get a good night's sleep, wake up on time, show up to work freshly shaved and on time, maintain a positive attitude, and be ready to face another day of potential challenges. This relentless cycle has often been mistaken for toughness.

However, true toughness in such demanding professions – be it in first response, professional athletics, the military, or medical fields – isn't about suppression or compartmentalization. It isn't about hiding the day's trauma from family or silently bearing the burden alone. Real toughness involves a two-fold approach: first, having the insight to recognize when an experience is affecting you emotionally and mentally, and second, having the courage to take proactive steps to address it. Toughness isn't about enduring pain in silence; it's about acknowledging your struggles and bravely seeking the support or help you need. True strength lies in vulnerability and the willingness to confront and process the emotional impact of such demanding work.

The Importance of Self-Assessment

I firmly believe in the power of self-assessment, and I encourage you to deeply consider this question: are you the same person now as you were before you started your current job? This question applies to everyone, whether you're a first responder or in another profession. Are you the same individual now as when you began your career?

Many people will answer no. But when asked about the reasons for this change, their responses almost always point to external factors. I've asked numerous police officers across the country this question. Often, they laugh and emphatically say no. When asked why, their explanations typically focus on external elements: administrative issues, societal changes, political climates, media portrayals, community support levels, and so on. Rarely, if ever, have I heard a first responder attribute this change to personal transformation. Responsibility is hard, especially when blaming and excusing are so readily available.

With all the compassion I possess, I want to emphasize that the primary change lies within you. The world is in a constant state of flux, always evolving and shifting. But the key shift that often goes unnoticed is the change in oneself. You forget "why" you were initially motivated. This phenomenon isn't unique to law enforcement; it's seen in nursing, teaching, the military, and virtually every profession. The crucial realization is that while the world changes around us, the most significant transformations occur within us. Remembering and reconnecting with your initial purpose and drive is essential to understanding and embracing these personal changes.

As I mentioned in the first chapter, one of my key recommendations for police departments nationwide (and I have so, so many) is to video record candidates and then have them watch their interviews once every year. This practice would serve as a powerful reminder of the passion and motivation they initially expressed.

By revisiting their original intentions and the enthusiasm they had when starting their journey, officers can maintain a strong connection to their core values and reasons for choosing this challenging but rewarding career path. This process would not only reinforce their commitment but also help them stay aligned with their original aspirations, often lost in the demanding and dynamic environment of first responder work.

When individuals embark on careers in public service, they often enter with bright eyes and a hopeful heart, driven by a desire to make a meaningful impact. However, they soon confront the harsh realities of systemic issues that pervade various sectors. The criminal justice system, behavioral health system, and healthcare system are all flawed, largely because they are human-made constructs, inherently imperfect and prone to errors.

Consider the journey of a nurse: after years of rigorous education and accumulating significant student loan debt with the noble intention of helping people, they often find themselves in hospital systems where the focus is skewed towards efficiency and profit rather than patient care. Nurses are pressured to rapidly turn over beds, reducing patient care to a mere transaction in the broader capitalist framework.

Similarly, first responders enter their fields with a vision of serving the community, only to become disillusioned by the systemic challenges within their organizations. They witness the prioritization of procedural efficiency over human-centered service, leading to frustration and a sense of disillusionment. They make good and lawful arrests, only to see the person walk out the door because a judge decides crime is okay sometimes.

This realization – that the institutions they joined to make a difference are flawed and often prioritize operational efficiency over human elements – can be deeply disheartening. It leads to a shift in perspective from idealistic aspirations to a more jaded view of the reality of their professions. This shift can result in a misplaced attribution of blame towards external factors rather than a reflective acknowledgment that perhaps it's their own perspectives and understanding that have evolved.

The cause of this is a disconnect between initial intentions and the eventual reality of working within these systems. It underscores the importance of maintaining a balance between operational necessities and the fundamental human aspect of these professions. For individuals in these roles, it's crucial to periodically reassess their motivations and perspectives, ensuring they don't lose sight of their original aspirations amid the systemic imperfections they navigate daily.

I recall a moment during an in-service class I was teaching when an officer approached me with a concern. He confided, "Joe, I don't think I'll make it to retirement." Initially, I assumed he was close to his retirement age, perhaps only a year or two away from it. He was an older gentleman, after all. But his response caught me off guard. "No, no," he clarified, "I just graduated last August." He was barely six months into the job.

For many, this revelation might prompt disbelief or even ridicule. People might wonder what was wrong with him or criticize his apparent lack of commitment. But my reaction was quite the opposite. I commended him. "Hey, man, good for you," I said.

This officer had successfully navigated the challenges required to enter the profession. This wasn't a small feat. He had endured what is known for being one of the longest police academies in the country, followed by a rigorous three-and-a-half-month field training program. And yet, only a few months into the job, he had the self-awareness to recognize that this path might not be right for him.

I have immense respect for anyone, first responder or otherwise, who makes the difficult decision of leaving a profession they have invested significant time and effort into, especially when they come to realize it's not aligning with their expectations or values. To make such a choice requires a level of honesty and courage that should be acknowledged and celebrated. Recognizing that a chosen path is not the right fit and then acting on that realization is commendable.

A lot of first responders I've met across the country truly hate their jobs. It is obvious they have lost their love for it. They can't stand where they work, they're fed up with their bosses, and they're just plain tired of dealing with people, yet they stick it out, thinking, *I've just gotta last another 15 years.* Think about the toll that takes on them, on their headspace and health – not to mention the impact on their families and the folks they serve.

When I ask them, "What's most important to you every day?" most will say, "My family, my kids." That sounds great, but is it even true? I've got a knack for getting under the skin of first responders because I've been there, done that. So, when I ask them about their top priority, and they say, "Family," I follow up with, "How much overtime are you working?" You see, there's a big gap here. They claim family is everything, but then they're the first to sign up for extra hours, which leads to avoiding the very thing they claim is most important.

If we dig deeper, they'll say they need the extra cash to give their family a better life. But I bet they never asked their kids what they wanted. Do their kids want more stuff, or do they just want more time with mom or dad? Chances are, the kids just want their parents around more, but we don't usually give them that choice. We rarely involve our children in our decision-making but instead do what we feel best.

It's crucial to step back and really think about what we're doing. Are we living true to what we say matters most? If we're always working, chasing that extra dollar, we might be missing out on what's genuinely important. And that's something we all need to think about – not just first responders, but all of us.

As parents, we often want to buy our kids stuff or do things for them. Deep down, it's because we're feeling insecure. We think that the more we give them, the better parents we are. In reality, this can end up straining us financially. As I dive into the six pillars of self-care, I want you to take a closer look at them. It doesn't matter what job you have; these pillars are part of learning how to put yourself first. The six pillars are physical, emotional, psychological, spiritual, personal, and professional self-care.

My hope for you as we go through each pillar is that you don't just focus on the stuff you're already doing. Instead, pay attention to the things you're not doing, especially the ones that make you feel uncomfortable or even annoyed. That's the exact thing I want you to try at least once. If something in these pillars rubs you the wrong way, ask yourself why. That reaction might point you toward something important that you've been avoiding or neglecting. Remember, the impediment to action advances action; the obstacle in the way becomes the way. The following portion of these six pillars is a high-level overview of each – something to get your mind going and thinking about. See how many you have done, are doing, or are willing to try. I would love to hear about it.

Physical Self-Care

The first pillar we will discuss is physical self-care. This includes visiting your primary care physician for an annual physical and getting your blood work checked to ensure everything's alright internally. Too often, especially for young adults, we believe if we are relatively healthy, feel good, eat something green, and work out sometimes – we are good to go and do not need an annual physical. This could not be further from the truth. The first step in becoming more selfish for selfless reasons is to get a physical, get bloodwork done, and see what is happening inside of your body. Then there's sleep – how much are you actually getting? You should aim for at least seven hours a night. Many people scoff at this idea, but that's because we've gotten too used to running on barely any rest. Operating on just four or five hours of sleep isn't something to be proud of; it can harm our health and effectiveness.

Food and diet are also crucial parts of this pillar. I admit, as someone with Italian heritage, I love my food way too much. I will eat pizza at least once a week for the rest of my life – pending any catastrophic events. But our relationship with food is complex. We often overeat during celebrations and times of sadness. Whether it's for a wedding, the Super Bowl, or a funeral, food is often more than just nourishment – it's both medicine and a drug. But we need to find the right balance in our eating habits. Again, this is not something I thrive at. And let's not forget exercise. Just like food, exercise is essential for maintaining our physical well-being. It's all about creating a balance that allows our bodies to function at their best.

I'm not your typical gym enthusiast; lifting weights isn't my thing. Never has been. However, put me in a game involving a ball – like basketball, soccer, tennis, pickleball, or golf – and I'm all in. Golf, in particular, is a favorite. I want to play golf five days a week, all over the country. I'll happily walk the course, especially if it's flat. It's important to recognize that exercise can come in many forms. What matters is finding an activity you enjoy that keeps you moving. According to the American Heart Association, you need about 150 minutes of physical activity a week. That comes down to moving your body at least 20 minutes a day to maintain good heart health. Obviously, a myriad of factors can impact this otherwise, but a brisk 20-minute walk a day, especially when paired with a balanced diet, is far greater for you than nothing at all.

Now, let's talk about massage and sports medicine. Regular massages are not just a luxury; they're a way to care for your body, helping with muscle recovery and stress relief. Physical intimacy is another aspect of physical self-care, and it's something I've come to understand better with time. Physical intimacy goes beyond just sex, especially for men. It's about closeness, connection, and touch in all forms.

I'm a 42-year-old man who only really grasped this concept at 37 after several failed marriages. My struggle has been understanding relationships and love – how to do them right. I used to blame my upbringing for my relationship issues, but I've come to accept that it's on me. I knew something was wrong but used physical intimacy as an escape. This lesson hit home in my current marriage, which started out long-distance. After we became physically intimate, there was an incident that really opened my eyes.

One day, we were just relaxing on the couch, watching TV, alone in the house. I reached out and gently touched her breast, thinking it was an intimate gesture. There I was, looking for connection, and she immediately pushed my hand away and got upset with me. That moment made me realize the depth and complexity of physical intimacy – it's not just about sex but about understanding and respecting each other's boundaries and comfort. I'm not ashamed to say that, all these years later, here I am, still struggling, still working through it all.

I thought she was just role-playing an angry woman when I casually touched her, but she wasn't pretending – she was genuinely upset. She told me, "You can't just touch my body whenever you want," and I was genuinely baffled. I argued, "But you're my girlfriend, and we've already had sex." To me, it seemed like a natural form of connection, not something to get upset about. But she felt differently, and because she cared, she informed my therapist about it. (Pause for laughter.)

At my next therapy session, my therapist brought up the incident and asked if I'd ever heard about non-sexual touch. I had no clue. She explained that women often appreciate gentle touches on the arm, back, shoulders, and hair. I blurted out, "What does that do for me?"

Her reaction was a facepalm, followed by, "Oh, my. We have a lot to work on."

I wasn't trying to be disrespectful or objectify my girlfriend. I was seeking intimacy and connection, something that set her apart from, say, a friend like Jesse, whom I wouldn't touch that way even after 24 years. This led me to learn about schema-focused therapy, which likens our experiences and responses to life to files in a cabinet. From birth, our needs and experiences – like the need to be fed, changed, or held – are filed away, much like in a card in a library card catalog before everything went digital.

How nostalgic. Do you remember card catalogs? They were little index cards directing you to the exact location of a book. Think of them as the schemas in our brains. To put it simply, as my therapist helped me understand, these schemas organize our experiences and responses from birth. As we grow and learn to crawl, gesture, cry to communicate – all these experiences get filed away.

However, when I was seven and endured sexual abuse, it was like someone opened my file drawer, threw my cards into the air, shuffled them around, crammed them back in, and then slammed the drawer shut. So, externally, I might've seemed normal, but my internal "card catalog" was in total disarray. All you had to do was look at my life to see this.

Fast forward to my relationship, where I thought a certain gesture was okay, but my partner found it problematic. We were on completely different pages. I'm still grappling with this, learning different ways to understand intimacy and its many layers.

One thing I've come to appreciate is the power of hugs. Science says the best way to hug is with two arms, chest to chest, for 23 seconds. It sounds odd, but hugging for more than 20 seconds releases oxytocin equivalent to a 60-minute workout – although, sadly, it won't help you lose weight. Trust me, I've tried.

Emotional Self-Care

Moving on to emotional self-care, we've got hobbies, cuddling with pets, community involvement, self-love, crying, and laughing. In my experience, one of the biggest issues with suicidal first responders and retirees is an identity crisis. Once their identity as a first responder is gone, they're left without a sense of self. It's a significant issue that needs addressing.

The second major issue I've observed, especially among retirees, is the lack of hobbies. Emotional self-care demands that we have hobbies. Life should be enjoyed; we should be having fun. Despite the seriousness and suffering in the world, finding joy in our activities is crucial. Personally, I love golf and make time for it whenever possible. I've also come to understand the difference between traveling and vacationing. For me, vacationing, the chance to relax and disconnect, is far more appealing. Traveling exhausts me – possibly because I am on the road nearly 25 days a month.

Cuddling with a pet can be soothing and release oxytocin, but human touch is also essential for our well-being. Community engagement goes beyond our professional duties. It's about selflessly giving our time, which can be incredibly rewarding and release dopamine. It's an integral part of self-care.

Self-love encompasses a range of activities, such as visiting the doctor, trying new foods, or taking trips. It's all about putting ourselves first. Lastly, the acts of crying and laughing are powerful. While most of us are comfortable with laughter, many, particularly men, struggle with expressing tears, especially in front of others. It's curious how we all recognize the human body's incredible capabilities but often forget that emotional expressions like crying are a natural and healthy part of our physiology.

We often accept everything our body naturally does – from needing to use the restroom after drinking water to sweating when we're hot or sneezing due to allergies. However, when it comes to crying, many of us resist this natural response. We fight back tears as if they diminish our humanity or masculinity. But I want to emphasize that if you feel the urge to cry, there's no shame in it. Let it out. Tears are just as natural and necessary as any other bodily function.

Psychological Self-Care

Psychological self-care is one of the areas I'm most passionate about. It involves spending time reflecting on our thoughts and experiences. This is where the value of therapy or coaching becomes apparent. I see them as two sides of the same coin. Therapy is beneficial for dealing with the past and addressing anything from yesterday or earlier. Coaching, on the other hand, is excellent for focusing on the present and future. It's about strategizing and planning for what lies ahead. Both therapy and coaching have their place in maintaining our psychological health, helping us process the past and navigate the path forward.

For meditation and mindfulness, I recommend setting aside just five minutes a day. Many people fear being alone with their thoughts, but mastering this fear through quiet reflection is powerful. A helpful tool I use is the Insight Timer app, which is free and excellent for practicing mindfulness and stillness. A great read on this topic is Ryan Holiday's *Stillness is the Key*.

Prioritizing stillness, not just during sleep but also when fully conscious, can significantly impact where our energy flows. Remember, energy follows attention. If you focus on negative thoughts, that's where your energy will gravitate. Conversely, finding beauty and gratitude can shift this dynamic. My daily gratitude practice involves asking myself three questions upon waking: Where am I? How did I get here? Who contributed to this? These questions ground me in the present and help me find gratitude in the moment, minimizing the sway.

I recommend journaling as part of your gratitude practice. Each day, jot down three things you're grateful for from the past 24 hours, ensuring they're always different. This practice helps keep your focus on the positive aspects of life, minimizing the sway of negative thoughts.

Psychological self-care also includes creative expression, such as painting, poetry, singing, and dancing. These artistic activities allow us to express ourselves in unique and fulfilling ways. Additionally, joining a group or a cause can reinforce community engagement, tying back to the importance of connecting with others and contributing to something larger than ourselves. These practices collectively contribute to a healthier, more balanced psychological state.

Spiritual Self-Care

I firmly believe that spirituality is a deeply personal journey, and there's no singular right path or belief system for everyone. My approach to spiritual self-care is not necessarily tied to a specific deity or religion. It's about finding what resonates with you on a personal and spiritual level.

My relationship with religion is unique and shaped by my experiences, despite having "Catholic" inscribed on my dog tags and permanently etched on my body. I never grew up attending church or practicing Catholicism. Moreover, I've had challenging experiences with religious guidance. For instance, during a particularly difficult phase in a previous marriage, a pastor at a Bible-based Christian church "guaranteed" me that my life would spiral out of control if I pursued a divorce. This advice came at a time when I was battling acute suicidal thoughts and striving to avoid a toxic home environment.

Contrary to the pastor's dire prediction, the six years since my divorce has been a period of significant improvement and growth. This experience highlights a critical issue: the danger of allowing others, even religious figures, to dictate our personal choices. It's important to remember that spirituality should empower us, not constrain us. Each person's spiritual journey is unique, and our choices should reflect our beliefs and experiences.

I wholeheartedly support seeking good counsel and believing in something larger than ourselves. However, it's crucial to avoid imposing our beliefs on others or making them feel invalidated in their spiritual journey.

So, what does spiritual self-care look like? It involves practices like forgiveness, spending time in nature, yoga, and volunteering – a theme that has recurred several times in this book. If you've never tried yoga before, give it a go. It's about much more than just the attire; it can bring significant benefits, especially with movements like Yoga for First Responders gaining traction.

Forgiveness is profoundly powerful. We've all experienced hurt in some form – being wronged, cheated, manipulated, or disrespected. Learning to forgive others is essential, but even more crucial is learning to forgive ourselves. We all carry something that we can forgive ourselves for, and acknowledging and addressing this can be incredibly liberating.

Personal Self-Care

On to personal self-care, which involves planning and setting goals. I'll share a framework I learned from Tom Bilyeu, which cost me around $5,000 for a four-week course. It focuses on critical decision-making in business, and the insights on goal-setting and achievement have transformed my life. In fact, this book is a testament to applying those lessons. I'll outline the model in detail, showing how it can be a powerful tool for realizing your ambitions and making significant changes in your life.

I want to share with you a principle that, if applied correctly, can help you achieve almost anything – provided it doesn't defy the laws of physics. Setting goals is the first step. Make them clear and incredibly specific. But remember, a lofty goal can only be achieved through the accumulation of micro goals. These micro goals gradually build micro habits, which, over time, evolve into significant, impactful habits. As you steadily accomplish these smaller objectives, you'll find yourself closer to your ultimate goal. Over time, with consistency, you will achieve whatever you set out to do.

Here is the formula: After you have detailed and written down your very specific goal, the immediate next step is to identify the block or impediment standing in your way. This is a concept from Marcus Aurelius and his famous quote, "The impediment to action advances action. What stands in the way becomes the way." This should be clear, concise, and explicit to achieving the goal you set for yourself. Now, once you have identified the impediment you must then create a hypothesis. Think of one thing, one task, one idea that could possibly get you closer to achieving your goal. Once you have your hypothesis formed, the next step is to test it. This can be done in many ways.

You could run a split test or A/B test. "A" is your controlled and original test, and "B" is your alternative variable or second variation. You could do a social proof test where you talk to 50 or 100 people, asking their opinions on whatever it is you are trying to unlock, create, learn, or achieve. The important part here is that you test, and test, and test until you can confidently say you have tested your hypothesis. The fourth step is to then measure the results of the testing you've done. And this part is easy. You ask yourself one simple question: Did the results from this test, created from my hypothesis, get me closer to my goal? If the answer is yes, you pour focused energy into that very thing, without quitting, until you accomplish your goal. If the answer is no, you simply go back to your hypothesis and realize it is not accurate. Create a new hypothesis, test it again, and measure the results until you get closer to your goal.

Understanding these five steps and putting them into action in my life and business has truly been life-changing.

1. Set a hyper-specific goal.
2. Identify the impediment.
3. Create a hypothesis.
4. Test, test, test.
5. Measure - if "yes," then pour into that thing. If "no," start back at #2.

Learning new skills is another crucial aspect. Skills are the great equalizers; they transcend race, gender, beliefs, and political affiliations. They simply don't discriminate. To paraphrase Oprah, become so skilled at something that you cannot be ignored. Remember, there will always be room for the top 1% in the top 1%.

Tony Robbins also offers a powerful insight: on the other side of your greatest fear lies your greatest breakthrough. Identify what's holding you back and confront it. For me, it was public speaking. Initially, I almost turned down applying for the Mental Health Unit because it involved teaching crisis intervention training. Now, looking back, it's ironic that my livelihood, supporting my family and the families of my team, comes from public speaking, conference keynotes, and training sessions. The very thing I feared most is now my source of income. This demonstrates how developing and honing skills can provide unimaginable opportunities. And always keep reading – ABR (Always Be Reading). Continuously learning and expanding your knowledge base can open doors you never knew existed.

To everyone reading this book, well done! You've made a fantastic choice. And if you're listening to the audiobook version, you failed miserably (HA!). Kidding! I am just pulling your leg hairs! Regardless of the format, the key is to always be learning. We should be constantly evolving, improving, and pushing ourselves to higher levels of knowledge and understanding, especially if we're aiming for greater achievements or success in our lives.

Spending quality time with friends is an essential part of personal self-care – emphasis on "quality" here. It's not just about being around people but investing time in meaningful interactions with those who enrich your life.

Think of your social circle as three parts of a whole. The first third should consist of mentors or those who have achieved goals similar to yours – they are the ones you look up to and learn from. The middle third comprises peers, people who are at a similar stage in life or career – your contemporaries. The final third should be those you mentor – those just starting in your field. This is your chance to give back and share the knowledge and experiences you've gained.

I'm quite open about my aspirations for financial success, not merely for my own benefit but to empower myself to assist others in ways that resonate with me. This approach transforms success into an instrument of kindness, allowing me to positively impact the lives of others. I've observed a common reluctance towards embracing financial prosperity, as if there's a widespread misunderstanding of capitalism and our roles within it. As Dave Ramsey said, "You cannot be radically generous without being radically wealthy."

Achieving financial milestones isn't about personal accolades; it's about crafting a legacy centered on aiding others. As my earnings have grown, I've consistently practiced giving back. Whether it's contributing to community projects, sponsoring initiatives, making donations, or investing in friends trying their hands at entrepreneurship, I'm committed to the philosophy of "doing good while doing well."

I firmly believe that the world reflects our actions, and by contributing positively, I've experienced a reciprocal bounty of blessings and opportunities. This cycle of goodwill has repeatedly affirmed itself, reinforcing the power of generosity and the impact of extending a hand to those around me. And I have seen the impact it has had on my children and how they see my generosity as a positive character trait.

Professional Self-Care

The final pillar we'll discuss is professional self-care. This is about breaking the monotony of your workday, whether it's stepping away from your desk or getting out of your patrol car during lunch. It's important to disrupt your usual routine periodically. Similarly, taking time off is more than just a break from work.

It's not about lounging at home with excessive eating, drinking, and sinking into the couch. Effective time off is about rejuvenation and refilling your energy reserves. It involves engaging in activities that help you unwind healthily and return to work refreshed, ideally to a job you love and find fulfilling.

Learning to say no to additional responsibilities, especially those that don't add value to your life, is an essential aspect of professional self-care. This includes declining extra shifts, side jobs, or projects that drain rather than fulfill you. A significant component of professional care is establishing personal and professional boundaries. Saying no is sometimes the necessary first step to overcoming the tendency to please others at your own expense.

It's also important to recognize that all of us, as part of our human experience, develop ways to cope or momentarily escape from our realities. Engaging in activities like watching Netflix for an extended period isn't inherently harmful. However, consistently resorting to such habits every time you're off work can indicate an unhealthy pattern. Professional self-care is about finding balance and understanding the reasons behind our behaviors, ensuring that our ways of unwinding are beneficial in the long run.

In this journey of self-improvement and self-care, I'm not suggesting there's a single correct way to live. The key is to regularly engage in self-reflection, asking yourself challenging questions. Assess where you are in life. Are you where you want to be? Do you feel how you aspire to most of the time? When you really look inward, how satisfied are you with yourself, your location, and how you're using your time, treasures, and talents?

Here's what I can assure you: if you commit to a few consistent practices, the change can be transformative. This isn't about one-off efforts but about embedding these practices into your daily life. First, seek professional help, such as therapy or life coaching. This should be from a professional, not just friends or family. Consistently engaging with someone trained to guide and support you can make a significant difference.

Next, start a gratitude practice. This can be formal or informal, but it should be a regular part of your routine. Reflect on the things you're thankful for each day. By doing this consistently, you cultivate a mindset that focuses on the positives in your life, which can profoundly influence your overall well-being and outlook.

When embarking on this journey of self-improvement and self-care, consider these five transformative practices not as occasional activities but as consistent daily habits. Dedicate at least five minutes each day to silence, embracing meditation or mindfulness. This commitment to inner stillness allows you to connect with your thoughts and feelings, paving the way for a calmer, more centered you.

Next, invest in learning something new or refining a skill you already possess. Consistent improvement in any area, whether a new hobby or a professional skill, not only enhances your abilities but also boosts your self-esteem and sense of accomplishment.

Volunteering is another vital component. Giving your time selflessly to a cause or organization you believe in is not just about helping others. It's a powerful way to enrich your own life, broaden your perspectives, and deepen your sense of purpose.

Reigniting Hope

If you commit to these practices regularly, imagine where you'll be in a year. Your life will likely have undergone a profound transformation. You might find that some people who were once fixtures in your life are no longer present, while you've attracted a new circle of individuals who align more closely with your evolved self. You will have cultivated a sphere of influence that reflects your new priorities and values.

These five practices are not just about being selfish in the traditional sense. They are about prioritizing your well-being, healing wounds, and creating a life that resonates with who you truly are. They are about making your well-being non-negotiable. By focusing on your personal growth and self-care, you not only enhance your life but also position yourself to contribute more effectively to the lives of those around you.

De-escalation skills and individual wellness are uniquely intertwined. If you lack competence in de-escalation, not only will it exacerbate challenging situations, but it can also significantly impact your mental equilibrium. Consider a scenario where tensions are escalating, either in a personal conflict or within oneself. In such instances, the absence of de-escalation skills escalates the conflict and contributes to heightened stress and a diminished sense of control.

Conversely, adeptness in de-escalation is a crucial component of mental health maintenance. Training this skill is like fortifying a mental resilience muscle; consistently applying calmness and composure in the face of adversity strengthens one's ability to recover from stressors more effectively. The skill defuses immediate tensions and enhances one's overall sense of well-being.

Back in my high school days, I watched an Oprah episode that left a lasting impression on me. Beyond her famous car giveaways, she shared a profound insight that really resonated with me. She mentioned the one thing she wished for everyone: hope. According to her, a lack of hope was a major contributor to people's suffering. That's the essence of this book – to reignite hope, even if it's just for a single individual.

I urge you to embrace the journey: take risks, heed your inner voice, pursue your passions, hone your skills, and believe in yourself. Don't shy away from nurturing your needs. Remember, we enter and exit this world alone, but our mission is to discover ourselves, live our best lives, love ourselves, and extend love, kindness, and compassion to others. There is no substitute for hard work and commitment to change, not sorry. I love you.

Afterword

It is important to reflect and consolidate the insights we've gained from this book. If enduring hardship is the price for maximizing our human potential and experience, then let's be kinder to ourselves. Life, in its inherent duality, will present us with plenty of challenges, but this means it will offer just as many opportunities. Despite our best efforts to align ourselves with societal or family expectations, we must acknowledge that life will forever remain unpredictable. We will all face pain, loss, illness, and death – they are inevitable parts of every life. But as Seneca said, "We suffer more often in imagination than in reality." Let's strive to minimize the sway of unprocessed emotions and unexamined thoughts.

If you find yourself grappling with the shadows of past hurt or unresolved suffering, recognize how these feelings manifest as behaviors. Then ask yourself, *Are these behaviors or habits serving me for good?* There is a good chance your unprocessed pain is hindering your growth and development as a leader (of your life, relationships, career, business, family, team, etc.). We must develop the courage to process these emotions constructively so we can transform them into a catalyst for positive change and both personal and professional development.

If this book has made an impact on you and you've found its lessons valuable, I'd be thrilled to connect further. I'm eager to bring these discussions to your organization, whether it's a group, agency, corporation, or a larger audience. My personal experiences and the insights and strategies I share can significantly enhance a variety of environments.

For those interested in deepening their personal and professional growth, SolutionPoint+ offers a range of tailored training programs. We also provide an online library featuring some of our most sought-after courses, perfect for those ready to invest in their development. These offerings are crafted to equip you with the necessary skills and knowledge to effectively handle life's challenges with empathy, resilience, and compassion.

May this book serve as a resource for you as you step into your light, overcome your fears, and awaken the spirit within that has been so eager to come out. Take care of yourself, love each other, and be well.

Website: www.solutionpointplus.com

Online Courses: https://go.solutionpointplus.com/

Free Offer

THANK YOU FOR READING MY BOOK!

Thank you for buying and reading my book. I would like to offer you a **FREE** online course for Effective Communication and Active Listening (*$97 value*).

To Download Your Free Video, Scan the QR Code: This will link you to an online video of the Effective Communication and Active Listening course.

I appreciate your interest in my book and value your feedback as it helps me improve future versions of this book. I would appreciate it if you could leave your invaluable review on Amazon.com with your feedback. Thank you!